INTELLIGENCE AND COUNTERINTELLIGENCE STUDIES

FEDERAL INTELLIGENCE SPENDING

ELEMENTS AND CONSIDERATIONS

INTELLIGENCE AND COUNTERINTELLIGENCE STUDIES

Additional books in this series can be found on Nova's website under the Series tab.

Additional e-books in this series can be found on Nova's website under the e-book tab.

INTELLIGENCE AND COUNTERINTELLIGENCE STUDIES

FEDERAL INTELLIGENCE SPENDING

ELEMENTS AND CONSIDERATIONS

ADALINE CORTEZ
EDITOR

Novinka
New York

For permission to use material from this book please contact us:
Telephone 631-231-7269; Fax 631-231-8175
Web Site: http://www.novapublishers.com

Additional color graphics may be available in the e-book version of this book.

Library of Congress Cataloging-in-Publication Data

ISBN: 978-1-63117-037-9

Published by Nova Science Publishers, Inc. † New York

CONTENTS

Preface		**vii**
Chapter 1	Intelligence Spending and Appropriations: Issues for Congress *Marshall C. Erwin and Amy Belasco*	**1**
Chapter 2	Intelligence, Surveillance, and Reconnaissance (ISR) Acquisition: Issues for Congress *Marshall Curtis Erwin*	**27**
Chapter 3	Intelligence Issues for Congress *Marshall Curtis Erwin*	**63**
Index		**101**

PREFACE

Appropriations for intelligence activities represent a significant part of both the federal and defense budget at a time of growing fiscal austerity. In the past, spending levels for intelligence activities were shrouded in secrecy. Today, overall totals of intelligence spending are made public, but the process for appropriating funds for intelligence activities remains complicated and not well understood. This book discusses the historic trend in intelligence spending, provides a broader issue concerning the intelligence budgeting process, and discusses intelligence issues for Congress.

Chapter 1 - It is now publicly acknowledged that intelligence appropriations are a significant component of the federal budget, over $78 billion in FY2012 for both the national and military intelligence programs. Limited publicly available data suggest intelligence spending, measured in constant 2014 dollars, has roughly doubled since the September 11, 2001, terrorist attacks and, before declines over the last three years, was almost double spending at its peak at the end of the Cold War. The recent disclosure by the *Washington Post* of details from the Administration's FY2013 National Intelligence Program (NIP) budget request may spark further debate about intelligence spending. It is likely that Members of Congress will more closely examine intelligence programs to ensure they are both effective and affordable. Perhaps the most important questions for Members are how and to what extent intelligence spending, after a decade of sharp growth, should fall in comparison to declines in other defense spending. See the section titled "Comparison with National Defense Spending" for further discussion on that topic.

Fiscal pressures today will require intelligence officials to more clearly establish priorities and to make difficult choices between different intelligence collection platforms and agencies. Such choices may not have been required during the past decade, during which additional funding could be found to address new threats and to fix organizational weaknesses. In the 1990s, during a previous round of budget cuts and prior to the establishment of the Director of National Intelligence (DNI), it was argued that the intelligence community lacked a rigorous system to establish priorities and to tailor the intelligence budgets to meet those priorities. It remains unclear whether intelligence reforms after September 11, 2001, sufficiently addressed this issue.

Intelligence spending is spread across the 17 organizations comprising the intelligence community. Over 90% of NIP funding, which focuses on strategic needs of decision makers and is notionally under DNI control, falls within the Department of Defense (DOD) budget. DOD members of the intelligence community also receive funding for tactical intelligence from the Military Intelligence Program (MIP), which is under the authority of the Secretary of Defense but which may fund intelligence collection platforms that could be used for both tactical and strategic purposes. The remaining portions of the NIP fall within several other Cabinet departments and two independent agencies. These overlaps complicate both budget formulation and the congressional appropriation process.

The appropriations process for intelligence activities is complex and not widely understood. A number of changes have been proposed that would streamline the process or disentangle the NIP from the Department of Defense budget.

Some, such as the proposal by a 9/11 Commission to combine authorization and appropriation responsibilities in a single committee, would be inconsistent with congressional practices during the past century. Other proposals to separate intelligence appropriations from defense appropriations, or to establish a separate intelligence title within defense appropriations acts, are less radical, but have met with opposition.

As a result, the congressional intelligence appropriations process is likely to receive continued attention. Congress may choose to review the DNI budget formulation process and appropriations procedures to ensure that they maximize effective decision making at a time when both national budgets and international threats to the United States remain issues of major public concern.

Chapter 2 - Increasing calls for intelligence support and continuing innovations in intelligence technologies combine to create significant challenges for both the executive and legislative branches. Intelligence, surveillance, and reconnaissance (ISR) systems are integral components of both national policymaking and military operations, including counter-terrorism operations, but they are costly and complicated and they must be linked in order to provide users with a comprehensive understanding of issues based on information from all sources. Relationships among organizations responsible for designing, acquiring, and operating these systems are also complicated, as are oversight arrangements in Congress. These complications have meant that even though many effective systems have been fielded, there have also been lengthy delays and massive cost overruns. Uncertainties about the long-term acquisition plans for ISR systems persist even as pressures continue for increasing the availability of ISR systems in current and future military operations and for national policymaking.

These challenges have been widely recognized. A number of independent assessments have urged development of "architectures" or roadmaps setting forth agreed-upon plans for requirements and acquisition and deployment schedules. Most observers would agree that such a document would be highly desirable, but there are significant reasons why developing such an architecture and gaining an enduring consensus remain problematic. First, ISR technologies are not static; whereas it is possible to plan for aircraft, ships, or tanks that can be used for decades, it is doubtful that today's inventory of satellites, unmanned aerial vehicles, and manned aircraft will still be the right mix a few years hence. Some believe that a "cast-in-concrete" plan would inhibit the ability to take advantage of new technologies or techniques as they emerge. Secondly, achieving consensus on such a plan would be greatly affected by the separate priorities of different parts of the intelligence community, the Defense Department, and Washington policymakers. The needs of policymakers and military commanders are different and are usually reconciled only on a case-by-case basis. Furthermore, different congressional oversight committees may also have different perspectives on priorities and some may seek to emphasize funding for specific systems.

The Director of National Intelligence could be given authority to reach across current organizational boundaries to define requirements and priorities. Some propose establishing a position for a separate "ISR Czar" to do this. Few observers believe that ISR programs could be carved out of the intelligence budget and/or the defense budget, and placed under the control of a single officer or lead agency. There is a strong likelihood that separate needs and concerns that affect the current systems will not disappear, even if one official has a new and expansive charter. Similar concerns would exist in regard to the jurisdictions of congressional oversight committees.

ISR issues will continue to be an area of concern for the 113th Congress, especially in light of the lack of a long-term investment strategy and the pending impact of sequestration. In testimony before the Senate Select Committee on Intelligence in March 2013, Director of National Intelligence James Clapper indicated that sequestration would delay major systems acquisition and require older reconnaissance systems to be decommissioned. The DNI and the President's FY2014 budget request indicated an effort to protect the intelligence community workforce, suggesting that hard choices in response to budget cuts will focus on ISR systems and other expensive collection platforms.

Chapter 3 - To address the challenges facing the U.S. intelligence community in the 21st century, congressional and executive branch initiatives have sought to improve coordination among the different agencies and to encourage better analysis. In December 2004, the Intelligence Reform and Terrorism Prevention Act (P.L. 108-458) was signed, providing for a Director of National Intelligence (DNI) with authorities to manage the national intelligence effort. The legislation also established a Director of the Central Intelligence Agency (CIA).

Making cooperation effective presents substantial leadership and managerial challenges. The needs of diverse intelligence "consumers" must all be met, using many of the same systems and personnel. The DNI has substantial statutory authorities to address these issues, but the organizational relationships remain complex, especially for intelligence agencies that are part of the Defense Department. Members of Congress in their oversight role may seek to observe the extent to which effective coordination is accomplished.

The intelligence community, which comprises 17 agencies, has experienced a decade of budgetary growth. That era was typified by (1) institution building with embryonic organization such as the Office of the DNI and other new or evolving intelligence components, (2) information sharing and collaboration across those institutions, and (3) a focus on counterterrorism.

While those issues will remain areas of congressional interest, Members will likely confronted by a new set of intelligence challenges resulting from budgetary realities and from second-order effects stemming from post-9/11 changes. These include:

- Consolidation and redundancy. Intelligence collection systems are expensive and some critics suggest there have been elements of waste and unneeded duplication of effort. The Administration is considering long-term reductions with an emphasis on potentially redundant information technology systems. There is great concern, however, that any reductions be carefully made to avoid curtailing capabilities that have become integral to military operations and to policymaking in many areas.
- Information security and management. The WikiLeaks disclosures that began in 2010 and other recent incidents of unauthorized disclosure of classified information have drawn considerable attention to the risks that widespread information sharing entails. Investigations into the 2009 Christmas day bombing attempt and the Fort Hood shooting also suggest analysts are now challenged to synthesize the large volumes of information being shared.
- Intelligence support to counterterrorism and operations. The Administration's targeting killing program raises legal, jurisdictional, and efficacy issues. Broader questions have also been raised about whether intelligence agencies have become too focused on counterterrorism to the detriment of other national security priorities and whether some of those functions should be transitioned to U.S. military control, allowing intelligence agencies to focus on traditional collection and analysis.

In: Federal Intelligence Spending
Editor: Adaline Cortez

ISBN: 978-1-63117-037-9

Chapter 1

INTELLIGENCE SPENDING AND APPROPRIATIONS: ISSUES FOR CONGRESS*

Marshall C. Erwin and Amy Belasco

SUMMARY

It is now publicly acknowledged that intelligence appropriations are a significant component of the federal budget, over $78 billion in FY2012 for both the national and military intelligence programs. Limited publicly available data suggest intelligence spending, measured in constant 2014 dollars, has roughly doubled since the September 11, 2001, terrorist attacks and, before declines over the last three years, was almost double spending at its peak at the end of the Cold War. The recent disclosure by the *Washington Post* of details from the Administration's FY2013 National Intelligence Program (NIP) budget request may spark further debate about intelligence spending. It is likely that Members of Congress will more closely examine intelligence programs to ensure they are both effective and affordable. Perhaps the most important questions for Members are how and to what extent intelligence spending, after a decade of sharp growth, should fall in comparison to declines in other defense

* This is an edited, reformatted and augmented version of a Congressional Research Service publication, CRS Report for Congress R42061, prepared for Members and Committees of Congress, from www.crs.gov, dated September 18, 2013.

spending. See the section titled "Comparison with National Defense Spending" for further discussion on that topic.

Fiscal pressures today will require intelligence officials to more clearly establish priorities and to make difficult choices between different intelligence collection platforms and agencies. Such choices may not have been required during the past decade, during which additional funding could be found to address new threats and to fix organizational weaknesses. In the 1990s, during a previous round of budget cuts and prior to the establishment of the Director of National Intelligence (DNI), it was argued that the intelligence community lacked a rigorous system to establish priorities and to tailor the intelligence budgets to meet those priorities. It remains unclear whether intelligence reforms after September 11, 2001, sufficiently addressed this issue.

Intelligence spending is spread across the 17 organizations comprising the intelligence community. Over 90% of NIP funding, which focuses on strategic needs of decision makers and is notionally under DNI control, falls within the Department of Defense (DOD) budget. DOD members of the intelligence community also receive funding for tactical intelligence from the Military Intelligence Program (MIP), which is under the authority of the Secretary of Defense but which may fund intelligence collection platforms that could be used for both tactical and strategic purposes. The remaining portions of the NIP fall within several other Cabinet departments and two independent agencies. These overlaps complicate both budget formulation and the congressional appropriation process.

The appropriations process for intelligence activities is complex and not widely understood. A number of changes have been proposed that would streamline the process or disentangle the NIP from the Department of Defense budget.

Some, such as the proposal by a 9/11 Commission to combine authorization and appropriation responsibilities in a single committee, would be inconsistent with congressional practices during the past century. Other proposals to separate intelligence appropriations from defense appropriations, or to establish a separate intelligence title within defense appropriations acts, are less radical, but have met with opposition.

As a result, the congressional intelligence appropriations process is likely to receive continued attention. Congress may choose to review the DNI budget formulation process and appropriations procedures to ensure that they maximize effective decision making at a time when both national budgets and international threats to the United States remain issues of major public concern.

INTRODUCTION

Appropriations for intelligence activities represent a significant part of both the federal and defense budget at a time of growing fiscal austerity. In the past, spending levels for intelligence activities were shrouded in secrecy. Today, overall totals of intelligence spending are made public, but the process for appropriating funds for intelligence activities remains complicated and not well understood. Steady, yearly increases in intelligence funding in the past decade helped create an intelligence apparatus that, many experts agree, has been effective at accomplishing its ultimate goal of preventing another terrorist attack on the scale of 9/11. But in the new era of fiscal limits, intelligence officials and Members of Congress are addressing ways to reduce intelligence spending while ensuring continued effectiveness against al-Qaeda and while adapting to new priorities other than counterterrorism. Director of National Intelligence (DNI) James R. Clapper Jr. recently stated that sequestration would require a 7% cut, or roughly $4 billion, to the National Intelligence Program (NIP) budget and warned of reduced global coverage and decreased human and technical intelligence collection. Mr. Clapper also warned of repercussions similar to those that occurred in the 1990s when, in concert with a one-third decrease in active duty military personnel, the intelligence community saw a 23% cut in its budget, resulting in what he characterized as a "damaging downward spiral."[1] The *Washington Post* on August 29, 2013, published details about the Administration's FY2013 NIP budget request, based on a document provided by former NSA contractor Edward Snowden. Because the document leaked to the news media is classified, CRS is unable to provide a discussion of the specific detail of that budget submission. Nonetheless, the disclosure may drive further public debate about the size of the intelligence budget and about the effectiveness of intelligence spending. This report discusses the historic trend in intelligence spending, as well as broader issues concerning the intelligence budgeting process, and may help Members of Congress contextualize information concerning the FY2013 budget.

INTELLIGENCE SPENDING: AN OVERVIEW AND TRENDS

Total intelligence spending can be understood as the combination of (1) the NIP, which covers the programs, projects, and activities of the intelligence community oriented towards the strategic needs of decision makers, and (2) the Military Intelligence Program (MIP), which funds defense intelligence activity intended to support tactical military operations and priorities.[2] Later sections of this report describe these programs in more detail. It is important to recognize that public comments about intelligence spending do not always distinguish between the NIP, the MIP, and the total of the two, complicating discussions on a subject about which there are already few details.

The 9/11 Commission recommended that the amount of money spent on national intelligence be released to the public.[3] In accordance with the Implementing the Recommendations of the 9/11 Commission Act, the Director of National Intelligence (DNI) in 2007 began to announce each year the amount of money appropriated for the NIP.[4] The Intelligence Authorization Act of 2010 also required the President to publicly disclose the amount requested for the NIP in his budget.[5] The Secretary of Defense began to release annual MIP appropriations figures in 2010 and specified those figures back to 2007.[6] These actions have provided public access to previously classified budget numbers for national and military intelligence efforts. *Table 1* provides these recently released figures in both nominal and constant 2014 dollars. Unless otherwise noted, values in this report are in constant dollars.[7]

Trends in Recent Years

Table 1. Intelligence Spending, FY2007-FY2013
In Billions of Nominal and Constant 2014 Dollars

		2007	2008	2009	2010	2011	2012	2013 requested	FY2013-FY2010
	Nominal	43.50	47.50	49.80	53.10	54.60	53.90	52.60	-.50
NIP									
	Constant	49.25	52.56	54.41	57.43	57.84	56.07	53.60	-3.83
	Nominal	20.0	22.90	26.40	27.00	24.00	21.50	19.20	-7.80
MIP									
	Constant	22.64	25.34	28.84	29.20	25.42	22.37	19.56	- 9.64
	Nominal	63.50	70.40	76.20	80.10	78.60	75.40	71.80	-8.30
Total									
	Constant	71.90	77.90	83.25	86.63	83.26	78.44	73.16	- 13.47

Sources: DNI & DOD press release.

Notes: Constant figures are deflated using the GDP index. Table 5-1 of DOD's National Defense Budget Estimate for FY2014, available at http://comptroller. defense.gov /defbudget/fy2014/FY14_Green_Book.pdf, provides a GDP price index with 2014 as the base year. Figures for 2013 are as requested by the President, without adjustment for sequestration.

Appropriations for intelligence activities amounted to over $78 billion in FY2012, the last year for which there is complete data.[8] The President's budget requested $73 billion for FY2013.[9] This does not take into account sequestration, and actual appropriated amounts are not yet available for 2013. Since peaking in 2010, total intelligence spending has fallen by at least 15%, which largely reflects a decrease in military intelligence spending.

The NIP and MIP figures above include funding for Overseas Contingency Operations (OCO)— roughly $10 billion annually for intelligence activities. It can be useful to distinguish OCO funding, including OCO funding for military intelligence, from other defense spending because that funding pays for wartime-related activities that differ from activities funded by the DOD base budget. For broader intelligence spending in the NIP, however, it is not clear what activity is supported by NIP OCO funds or to what extent that activity is qualitatively different than other intelligence operations taking place across the globe. *Figure 1* breaks out OCO funds from other MIP and NIP funding. Base budget intelligence spending grew by more than $10 billion, peaking in FY2010, while OCO intelligence spending grew by about $3 billion, peaking in FY2011.[10]

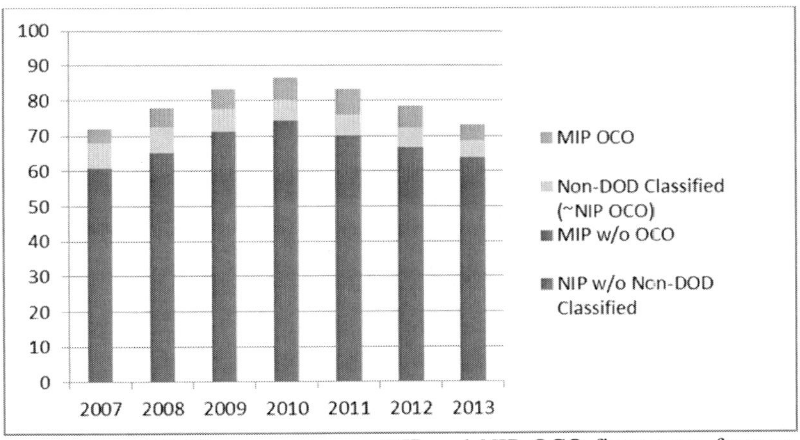

Sources: DNI and DOD press releases. MIP and NIP OCO figures are from yearly OCO budget requests available through the DOD Comptroller.

Notes: Deflated using the GDP index. Figures for 2013 are as requested by the President, without adjustment for sequestration.

Figure 1. Total Intelligence Spending, FY2007-FY2013. (In Billions of 2014 Dollars).

Policy makers have remarked that intelligence spending has doubled since September 11, 2001.[11] CRS analysis suggests that the NIP slightly more than doubled in real terms from 2001 to 2012 while the MIP grew at a slower pace. The NIP budget in 2001 (then referred to as the National Foreign Intelligence Program—NFIP) was roughly $24 billion in constant 2014 dollars, or less than half of the NIP budget for FY2012.[12] After sequestration, the NIP budget from 2001 to 2013 will have roughly doubled.[13] Publicly available data suggest the total intelligence budget in FY2001 was roughly $37 billion, or almost half of the $78 billion intelligence budget for FY2012.[14]

Trends Since 1980

Total intelligence spending previously peaked in 1989, at 125% above spending in 1980, before declining in the mid-1990s to 80% above spending in 1980.[15] It is possible to estimate that total intelligence spending in 1980 was slightly less than $21 billion, in current dollars. Spending appears to have quadrupled between 1980 and 2010 before declining over the past three years. These estimates are based on information provided by the 1996 Commission on the Roles and Capabilities of the U.S. Intelligence Community, which described the trend in intelligence spending from 1980 to the mid-1990s and the projected spending trend from the mid-1990s to 2001. The commission specified the percentage change at key points in time but not actual spending levels. The Director of Central Intelligence (DCI) also publicly disclosed the amount appropriated for intelligence for FY1997 and FY1998. Using the trends described by the commission and the figure for FY1997, CRS estimated spending in 1980 and 1989.[16] The methodology for the estimates is further explained in the "notes" below *Figure 2*. Both the DCI disclosures and the commission appear to combine national and military intelligence spending.[17] Data are not available specifically for national intelligence over this extended timeframe.

Comparison with National Defense Spending

The vast majority of intelligence spending falls within the national defense function—the budget category that includes the military activities of DOD as well as other national security activities. Using the estimates above, it is possible to separate total intelligence spending from the national defense function and to compare the growth in intelligence spending to the growth in national defense spending without intelligence.[18] Total intelligence spending grew more sharply than other national defense spending in both the 1980s and after 2001.

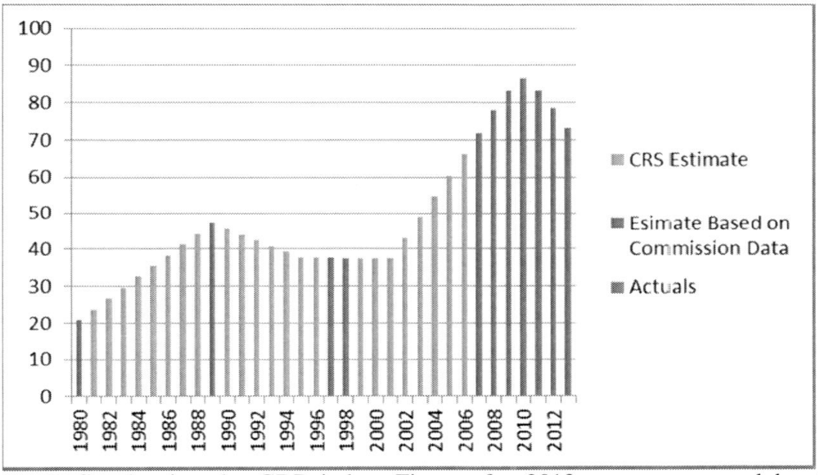

Notes: Deflated using the GDP index. Figures for 2013 are as requested by the President, without adjustment for sequestration. For 1980 and 1989, estimates use data provided by the 1996 Commission on the Roles and Capabilities of the U.S. Intelligence Community, coupled with total intelligence spending figures provided for FY1997. The commission indicated that "total intelligence funding grew by 125% in real (constant dollar) terms from 1980 to 1989 but declined thereafter to its current level of 80% above 1980." Total intelligence spending in FY1997 can therefore be used to estimate spending in 1989 and 1980. Because the commission indicated that spending was projected to remain flat or decrease from the mid-1990s through 2001, CRS estimates from 1995 to 2001 are derived by using figures for FY1997 and FY1998 and adjusting for inflation. The graph assumes equal yearly increases and decreases to estimate intelligence spending between 1980 and 1989, between 1989 and 1995, and between 2001 and 2007. For additional information, see page 131 of the commission's report, available at http://www.gpo.gov/fdsys/pkg/GPO-INTELLIGENCE/pdf/GPO-INTELLIGENCE-17.pdf.

Figure 2. Estimated and Actual Total Intelligence Spending Since 1980. (In Billions of 2014 Dollars).

As noted, total intelligence spending previously peaked in 1989, at 125% above spending in 1980, before declining in the mid-1990s to 80% above spending in 1980. In comparison, national defense excluding intelligence grew by 55% from 1980 to its peak in 1985 before declining in the mid-1990s to roughly equal that in 1980. As shown in *Figure 2,* total intelligence spending grew by about 110% from 2001 to 2012. National defense excluding intelligence grew by 55% over that time period. As a result of these trends, when measured from 1980, total intelligence spending by 2012 had grown 274%, while national defense spending without intelligence had grown 82% over that time period.

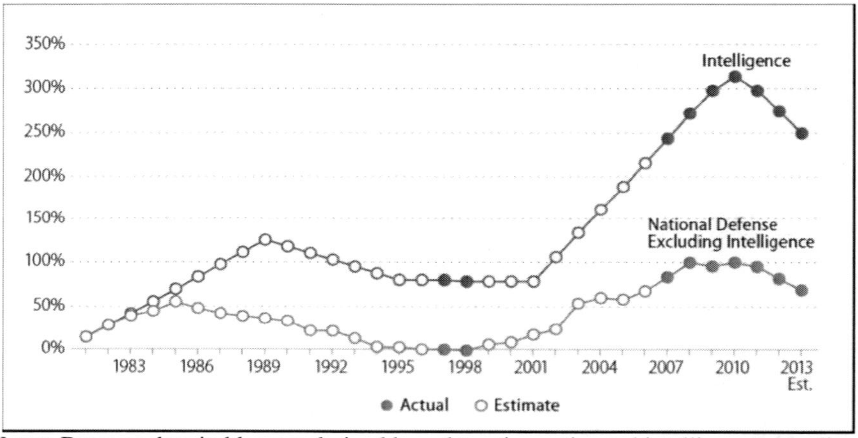

Notes: Because data in blue are derived by subtracting estimated intelligence spending, using the methodology described in Figure 2, from actual national defense spending, those figures are also estimates. See footnote 18 for further detail.

Figure 3. Intelligence Compared with National Defense Spending. (Real percentage change from 1980).

Perhaps one of the most critical questions facing Congress is whether intelligence spending will fall in concert with other defense spending. Some argue that as defense spending decreases, intelligence spending should remain flat or rise because a robust intelligence apparatus would be necessary to compensate and provide forewarning to a smaller, more nimble DOD. While plausible, this argument belies the fact that, as demonstrated by **Figure 3**, intelligence spending has already been decoupled from defense spending—the two in recent decades have tended to move in the same direction but have changed by different degrees.

Another argument about the relationship between defense and intelligence spending concerns the diversity and magnitude of the threats to U.S. interests.

Intelligence spending might appropriately be correlated to the diversity of threats. The intelligence community has argued that, especially after September 11, 2001, the range and complexity of threats to the United States has expanded to include not only state actors, but also non-state actors involved in activities such as terrorism, cyber-attacks, and drug trafficking. To fulfill the strategic needs of decision makers, the community must to some degree dedicate resources towards those threats. In comparison, while DOD must do contingency planning to address a diversity of threats, it does not necessarily need to dedicate resources towards each of them. Further, the cost to DOD of addressing new threats may not be as large as the cost associated with challenges from traditional state actors like the Soviet Union. Defense spending might thus be understood to correlate to the total size of the threat to U.S. interests.

Hence, this would explain and to some extent justify the divergence of intelligence spending from other national defense spending since the end of the Cold War, when many experts agree the number of threats to U.S. interests multiplied even while the sheer magnitude of the threat may have decreased. The question remains whether, after a decade of sharp growth and after the most critical improvements to intelligence capabilities have by some accounts already been made, intelligence spending can now be pared back while preserving necessary tools and capabilities.

Developing and Enforcing Intelligence Spending Priorities

DNI James R. Clapper, in March 2013 testimony before the Senate Select Committee on Intelligence, stated that "in my almost 50 years in intelligence, I do not recall a period in which we've confronted a more diverse array of threats, crises and challenges around the world.... Threats are more interconnected and viral."[19] The challenge for Congress and the intelligence community in light of this assessment may be to better establish priorities and to align relevant budgets accordingly. Absent such a process, resources may not be focused on the most critical issues, making it difficult to respond effectively to the myriad threats that the intelligence community argues are in need of attention.

During a previous round of budget cuts in the 1990s and prior to the establishment of the DNI, some critics argued that the intelligence community lacked a rigorous system to establish priorities and to shape the intelligence budgets to meet those priorities. The intelligence community at the time was overseen by the Director of Central Intelligence, who also served as the head of the Central Intelligence Agency (CIA) and who many argue was too focused on the CIA, to the detriment of his broader duties. This by some accounts made it difficult to adapt to the new fiscal realities of the 1990s when spending fell in response to the dissolution of the Soviet Union.

A 1996 report from the Council on Foreign Relations questioned the role of intelligence community management in priority setting, stating that, "Intelligence requirements are most often set by intelligence producers or by relatively junior officials in the policymaking departments."[20] The 1996 Commission on the Roles and Capabilities of the United States Intelligence Community found that not only were requirements often set by lower level staff, but any guidance from the DCI may often have come too late in the process to affect program priorities:

> The [Director of Central intelligence] is charged by law to "provide guidance to elements of the Intelligence Community for the preparation of their annual budgets." Usually, this guidance is issued by the DCI's staff or jointly with the Office of the Secretary of Defense after an overall level of funding has been decided by the Secretary of Defense and the DCI, and takes into account presidentially directed needs and priorities, statements of national security strategy, analyses of intelligence "gaps" and future needs, and other pertinent direction. Often, however, this guidance comes after the program and budget process has begun, and the program managers have already incorporated their own assumptions about intelligence requirements into budget estimates.[21]

Similarly, a House Permanent Select Committee on Intelligence (HPSCI) report from 1996 referred to a problem of the "tail trying to wag the dog," with respect to the intelligence budget process, meaning that community-level staff would compile the budget proposals of different agencies but exercised little oversight or control over those budgets.[22] Thus, individual intelligence community components were able to establish their intelligence priorities and to shape their budgets to meet those priorities without effective overall rationalization of effort. Some observers believed the community-level staff under the DCI lacked sufficient authority and insight into the budget of individual agencies while others believed the DCI had significant budgetary authority that he never used effectively.

In part because of the concerns above, the Intelligence Reform and Terrorism Prevention Act of 2004 created the DNI and arguably expanded its budgetary authorities beyond those previously possessed by the DCI. While the act stated that the DNI would "develop and determine an annual consolidated National Intelligence Budget," that language almost matched the budget formulation authorities granted to the DCI. However, the 2004 law also granted the DNI additional reprogramming authority and the means to monitor and execute the NIP, authorities the DCI lacked.[23]

Since 2004, the DNI has adopted two primary administrative mechanisms to establish intelligence priorities and then allocate resources towards those priorities, the National Intelligence Priorities Framework (NIPF) and the Intelligence Planning, Programming, Budgeting, and Evaluation (IPPBE) process.

The National Intelligence Priorities Framework

The NIPF, which was developed under the DCI and adopted by the DNI in 2005, is the process by which the DNI identifies intelligence topics relevant to policy makers and assigns priorities to intelligence targets based on those topics. The NIPF is designated as "the DNI's sole mechanism for establishing national intelligence priorities."[24]

Members of the intelligence community are directed to allocate collection and analytic resources in accordance with the NIPF. The DNI Chief Financial Officer is responsible for ensuring that NIP resources are allocated towards priorities identified in the NIPF.[25] However, some have questioned the effectiveness of this process.

Ambassador Robert Hutchings, the chairman of the DNI's National Intelligence Council from 2003 to 2005, stated in a 2007 hearing before the House Permanent Select Committee on Intelligence that the NIPF was "little more than diplomatic or bureaucratic busywork."[26] A point to stress is that there is little publicly available information that would help corroborate or refute the Ambassador's claim.

The Intelligence Planning, Programming, Budgeting, and Evaluation

Intended to parallel DOD's programming and budgeting process, the IPPBE system is the budgetary mechanism used to develop the NIP. Of note, the intelligence community directive that describes the IPPBE does not mention the NIPF, suggesting the DNI's key mechanism for developing intelligence priorities might have a limited role in the budget formulation process.

The planning phase of the IPPBE does involve an analysis of intelligence community priorities and gaps, although how and to what extent the NIPF informs that analysis us unknown. After IPPBE analysis is completed by the DNI's staff, it is then used to provide programmatic guidance to members of the intelligence community, and such guidance should be reflected in responses provided to the DNI that are used to actually formulate the NIP.[27]

Potential Oversight Issues for Congress

Before the creation of the DNI, the reports discussed in the previous section suggested that administrative mechanisms intended to establish intelligence priorities were perfunctory exercises. Priorities and corresponding budget allocations reflected the priorities in individual agencies. Such was the situation prior to intelligence reform in 2004 and the establishment of a DNI with expanded budgetary authorities over the different components of the intelligence community.

Recently, observers have raised concerns that the intelligence community has become too focused on counterterrorism and support to the military, to the detriment of other, more strategic intelligence priorities. A press account published in early 2013 alleged that a classified report prepared by the President's Intelligence Advisory Board (PIAB) in 2012 found that, after a decade of counterterrorism and intelligence support to the wars in Iraq and Afghanistan, the CIA and other members of the intelligence community had become too focused on tactical operations.[28]

In light of these considerations and growing budgetary pressures, Congress may act to examine the NIPF and IPPBE processes to determine their effectiveness at shaping the NIP.[29] Possible oversight questions include:

- How and to what extent does the NIPF affect the collection and analytic priorities of individual agencies?
- Does the DNI's staff exercise its full authority over the budgets of individual intelligence agencies?
- To what extent do individual agencies incorporate the planning guidance from the DNI when formulating their budgets?
- After intelligence community components provide their budget proposals, to what extent does the DNI adjust budget submissions in accordance with intelligence community priorities?

THE INTELLIGENCE APPROPRIATIONS PROCESS

Intelligence appropriations are inherently complicated because of the nature of both the intelligence community and the budgeting and execution processes that have developed over time. Funds for the large national-level intelligence agencies—CIA, the National Security Agency (NSA), National Reconnaissance Office (NRO), National Geospatial Intelligence Agency (NGA), and Defense Intelligence Agency (DIA)—are included in the NIP and are generally believed to consume a large portion of annual intelligence funding.[30]

The NIP also includes funding for the State Department's Bureau of Intelligence and Research (INR) and intelligence efforts in other civilian agencies, including the Federal Bureau of Investigation (FBI) and the Departments of Justice, Commerce, and the Treasury. Funds for the intelligence components of the military departments are included in the MIP. In addition, the MIP includes some funds for the tactical intelligence activities of the NSA, NRO, NGA, and DIA.[31]

Agency	Funding Source	Primarily
		NIP/MIP
CIA	Defense Appropriations	NIP
INR	State and Foreign Operations Appropriations	NIP
NSA	Defense Appropriations	NIP
DIA	Defense Appropriations	NIP
NGA	Defense Appropriations	NIP
NRO	Defense Appropriations	NIP
Army Intelligence	Defense Appropriations	MIP
Navy Intelligence	Defense Appropriations	MIP
Air Force Intelligence	Defense Appropriations	MIP
Marine Corps Intel.	Defense Appropriations	MIP
Coast Guard Intel.	Homeland Security Appropriations	NIP
FBI	Commerce, Justice, Science Appropriations	NIP
DEA	Commerce, Justice Science Appropriations	NIP
Dept. of Energy	Energy and Water Appropriations	NIP
Dept. of the Treasury	Financial Services, General Government Appropriations	NIP
DHS	Homeland Security Appropriations	NIP

The DNI develops and determines the NIP budget and presents it to the President for his approval "together with any comments from the heads of departments containing agencies or organizations."[32] The President's annual budget is then submitted to Congress, normally in early February of each year.

Congress reviews the President's budgets and appropriates funds for intelligence mostly in defense appropriations legislation, which has always included the vast bulk of intelligence spending—probably well over 90% of the NIP. Appropriations for the CIA are included in defense appropriations acts, but are transferred directly to the Director of the CIA, and the Defense Department has no role in the apportionment or allocation of CIA funds. Funding for intelligence activities of some departments, namely State, Justice, Homeland Security, Energy, and the Treasury, is provided in other appropriations measures.

Once appropriations legislation (or a continuing resolution) is enacted prior to the beginning of the new fiscal year, the Office of Management and Budget (OMB) apportions funds to the various agencies with national intelligence programs based on the Administration request and congressional adjustments.

Reprogramming after Enactment

Reprogrammings and transfers are others tools that the DNI can use to manage intelligence resources by transferring funds to meet unanticipated, higher priority needs.[33]

The Intelligence Reform and Terrorism Prevention Act of 2004 provided the DNI with the authority to reprogram or transfer NIP funds to a higher priority intelligence activity, with the approval of the Director of the Office of Management and Budget and after consultation with the heads of affected agencies or organizations.[34] Cumulative reprogrammings or transfers out of any department or agency must be less than $150 million and less than 5% of the NIP budget for that department or agency. The DNI may exceed these limits with the concurrence of the relevant department head. In addition, the Consolidated Appropriations Act of 2012, (P.L. 112-74) and the Consolidated and Further Continuing Appropriation Act of 2013 (P.L. 113-6) stated that the DNI could transfer at most $2 billion of NIP funds appropriated for FY2012 and FY2013.[35]

PROPOSED CHANGES TO INTELLIGENCE APPROPRIATIONS

The complexities of the intelligence appropriations process have led to a number of proposals for different approaches that seek in various ways to disentangle national intelligence funding from the defense budget. Although the DNI has a statutory responsibility to manage NIP funds, the Office of the Secretary of Defense also has a major role in budget execution, to some extent sharing responsibility with the DNI. The Intelligence Reform Act provides that the DNI "shall be responsible for managing appropriations for the National Intelligence Program by directing the allotment or allocation of such appropriations,"[36] but also provides that this be done in a manner "that respects and does not abrogate the statutory responsibilities" of heads of departments.[37]

A key issue here is the potential for competing goals and different priorities that may derive from the respective roles of the DNI and the Secretary of Defense in preparing the annual budgets for intelligence agencies and for allocating appropriated funds for intelligence activities within national-level DOD agencies. The "does not abrogate" language creates a level of ambiguity regarding the respective budgetary authorities of the DNI and Secretary of Defense. While the DNI effectively has authority over the NIP today, in the event of major changes to the budgets of the DOD component of the intelligence community, this ambiguity in the statute could result in challenges to the DNI's stewardship of the intelligence community. Even absent such changes, the fact that much of the NIP is buried within the defense budget might complicate budget formulation and execution.

Some observers have suggested that intelligence appropriations should be separated from defense appropriations and that Congress should consider a separate appropriations act (or a separate title in a larger appropriations act) for intelligence. Others have suggested establishing separate intelligence appropriations subcommittees. Such approaches, proponents maintain, would provide a better opportunity for Congress to consider the national intelligence effort as a collective whole and give the DNI a greater role in ensuring that government-wide requirements are not sacrificed to meet the immediate needs of DOD programs. On the other hand, skeptics argue that these changes would provide the DNI no new insights that he cannot currently obtain, and that they would complicate ties between intelligence programs and closely related non-intelligence DOD programs such as satellite launch programs. Sections below discuss these proposals in more detail.

An Intelligence Title within Defense Appropriations Acts?

One option for policy makers would be for defense appropriations subcommittees, as presently constituted, to report a defense appropriation bill that would include a separate title for the NIP. Current defense appropriations bills include a Title VII, Related Agencies, that provides funding for the CIA Retirement and Disability System Fund and for the Intelligence Community Management Account (which includes the Office of the DNI and the National Counterterrorism Center (NCTC)).[38] A new title could be established, or Title VII could be expanded, to include all NIP funding, with corresponding reductions in other defense accounts. This approach would give greater visibility to NIP funding and would not necessarily require separate 302(b) allocations, which set limits for each appropriations subcommittee as part of the congressional budget process. A major advantage of this approach is that it would require fewer changes to the intelligence appropriations process compared to the two proposals discussed below.

A Separate Intelligence Appropriations Act?

The 9/11 Commission, in addition to recommending that amounts appropriated for national intelligence be disclosed, urged that "Congress should pass a separate appropriations act for intelligence, defending the broad allocation of how these tens of billions of dollars have been assigned among the varieties of intelligence work."[39] Overall amounts requested and appropriated are now made public.[40] This development arguably facilitates the preparation of a separate intelligence appropriations act.

The option of a stand-alone intelligence appropriations act would entail the separation of appropriations for the NIP from the DOD budget. Although not calling for a separate appropriations bill, DNI Clapper spoke favorably of separating the NIP from the DOD budget during his confirmation hearing as DNI in July 2010. Responding to a question from Senator Russ Feingold, DNI Clapper stated:

> I would support and I've also been working and have had dialogue with actually taking the National Intelligence Program out of the DOD budget since the reason, the original reason for having it embedded in the department's budget was for classification purposes. Well, if it's going to be publicly revealed, that purpose goes away. And it also serves the

added advantage of reducing the topline of DOD department budget, which is quite large, as you know and that's a large amount of money that the department really has no real jurisdiction over.[41]

Four months later, in November 2010, Mr. Clapper suggested that this would be the Administration's approach beginning with the budget submission for FY2013 that will be forwarded to Congress in February 2012.[42] However, DNI Clapper indicated in an address to the Geospatial Intelligence Foundation in October 2011 that the NIP would not be placed in a separate budgetary category under the DNI.[43] Although he provided no details regarding the decision, it is possible that concerns reflected in House-passed legislation may have affected the decision.

To improve tracking of the NIP, Section 433 of the FY2012 Intelligence Authorization Bill, H.R. 1892 (P.L. 112-87), which was signed by the President on January 3, 2012, permits the establishment of separate accounts in the Treasury to which intelligence funds could be transferred and separately accounted for.

This capability was advocated by DNI Clapper as a means to improve the management of the NIP in his September 2011 testimony. "Specifically, managing this program as a coherent whole would improve efficiency, transparency and accountability." He added at another point in the hearing that "it is a challenge to watch execution. And a lot of it is because we simply don't have the auditable tools in order to watch how the money's actually being spent."[44]

Separate Intelligence Appropriations Subcommittees?

Some suggest that a separate intelligence appropriations bill would call for a separate appropriations subcommittee for national intelligence. Both the House and Senate took steps in this direction, but ultimately neither established separate subcommittees for intelligence. A separate intelligence appropriations subcommittee would be given a separate budget allocation in accordance with Section 302(b) of the Congressional Budget Act that would limit spending levels in bills.[45] Furthermore, with a separate intelligence appropriations subcommittee, it would be difficult to shift intelligence funds to defense activities. This option would probably encounter opposition in Congress because it would require changes to the appropriations committee structure.

Caution in the House

Proposals for separating intelligence appropriations from defense appropriations or even initiatives to provide procedures for identifying intelligence programs have encountered significant congressional resistance in the past. In particular, language in the FY2012 defense appropriations bill, H.R. 2219, passed by the House in July 2011, appeared to prohibit efforts to separate the NIP from DOD funding. Section 8116 of H.R. 2219 provides that:

> None of the funds appropriated in this or any other Act may be used to plan, prepare for, or otherwise take any action to undertake or implement the separation of the National Intelligence Program budget from the Department of Defense budget.

A similar provision was not included in the version of the FY2012 defense appropriations bill that was reported in the Senate on September 15, 2011. However, this provision survived the conference committee and was included in H.R. 3671, the Consolidated Appropriations Act, 2012, which became law in January 2012 (P.L. 112-74). The same language was included in H.R. 933, the Consolidated and Further Continuing Appropriations Act, 2013, which became law in March 2013 (P.L. 113-6). The House version of the FY2014 National Defense Authorization Act (H.R. 1960) went further. The act precluded the use of DOD funds to move NIP out of the DOD budget, to consolidate the NIP budget within DOD, or to establish a new appropriations account for the NIP. The Senate has not yet passed its authorization act.

CONCLUSION

Specific proposals to change the intelligence appropriations process have been controversial. There is strong resistance to separate intelligence appropriations bills, and little attention has as yet been given to a separate title for the NIP within defense appropriations legislation. DNI Clapper has apparently dropped plans to separate the NIP from DOD's budget. Moreover, the intelligence oversight structure, which the 9/11 Commission characterized as "dysfunctional," has remained largely unchanged. Efforts to establish new congressional committees with both authorization and appropriations responsibilities appear to have generated little interest. A separate appropriations subcommittee for intelligence was approved by the Senate but never established, nor has the House created an entirely separate subcommittee. Thus, for the moment, Members of Congress have to work with existing intelligence appropriations and oversight mechanisms to help shepherd the intelligence community into a new fiscal era.

These issues also raise broader questions about the extent and sufficiency of DNI authorities, a topic of much debate in the years immediately following intelligence reform, especially as it related to the personnel and funding of the Department of Defense elements of the intelligence community. Regarding the proposal to move the intelligence community out of DOD's budget, DNI Clapper stated that it would give "ODNI a lot more authority and insight and transparency over [the NIP]," suggesting he currently lacks sufficient authority and insight.[46]

There currently appears to be little appetite for a debate about an expansion of DNI authorities, probably in part because of unanswered questions about the current remit and effectiveness of the Office of the DNI. Nonetheless, DNI authorities may be more critical now, when declining budgets force choices between different intelligence platforms and agencies, as opposed to when the DNI faced the relatively easy process of managing a decade of budgetary growth.

APPENDIX. ACTIONS TAKEN IN RESPONSE TO THE RECOMMENDATIONS OF THE 9/11 COMMISSION

The 9/11 Commission recommendations included a variety of changes intended to strengthen congressional oversight of intelligence and streamline the intelligence budgeting process. Responding to those recommendations about intelligence appropriations, Congress undertook a number of initiatives, but some measures have not been implemented and others have been reversed. None appears to have fundamentally altered the process.

House Initiatives

Both the House and Senate responded to the 9/11 Commission's recommendations to set up separate appropriations subcommittees for intelligence. H.Res. 35 of the 110th Congress established a Select Intelligence Oversight Panel within the House Appropriations Committee. The panel was to consist of not more than 13 Members of whom no more than 8 came from the same political party, including the chairman and ranking Member of the Appropriations Committee, the chairman and ranking Members of the defense appropriations subcommittee, six additional Members of the Appropriations Committee, and three Members of the intelligence committee. The select panel was established to:

> Review and study on a continuing basis budget requests for and execution of intelligence activities; make recommendations to relevant subcommittees of the Committee on Appropriations; and, on an annual basis, prepare a report to the Defense Subcommittee of the Committee on Appropriations containing budgetary and oversight observations and recommendation for use by such subcommittee in preparation of the classified annex to the bill making appropriations for the Department of Defense.

Proponents of H.Res. 35 indicated their determination to support the intent of the recommendations of the 9/11 Commission and pointed to three principal concerns:

> The first was that the intelligence authorizing committee was routinely ignored by the administration and the intelligence community because they didn't provide the money. In this town, people follow the money.
>
> Secondly, the Appropriations Committee, frankly, was negligent in its responsibilities for oversight ...
>
> The third problem that we faced is that there was grossly insufficient staff on the part of the Appropriations Committee to have decent congressional oversight. ...The other problem was that there was not sufficient emphasis on intelligence matters by the Defense Appropriations Subcommittee because they had a lot of other things to do.[47]

Opponents argued that the proposal did not significantly change the previously existing structure: "Rather than consolidating oversight authority into a single committee that has both authorizing and appropriating authority, it just creates a new committee that has neither, doesn't have either of those powers."[48]

In July 2008, the chairman of the panel, Representative Rush Holt, described the panel's recommendations to the Defense Appropriations Subcommittee, claiming that "in the course of a year and [a] half since the creation of this Panel we have directly influenced the intelligence fund for five bills. Three of these bills were supplemental appropriations and this is the second annual appropriations bill that we have acted upon." He indicated that the panel forwarded recommendations higher than the previous year's levels but lower than the Administration's request. The panel's recommendations sought, he maintained, to require the ODNI to better manage the budget and enhance the role of Congress in reviewing the budget request and overseeing the DNI's performance. Rush argued: "One of the problems of past Congressional oversight has been that the Intelligence Community was forced to cut or add programs based on the changing whims of Congress. The creation of this Panel and stronger budgetary oversight over intelligence programs will hopefully provide stability for our nation's intelligence professionals." Representative Holt also noted that the panel recommended changes to space programs and encouraged a robust investment in foreign language training.[49]

In January 2011, the 112th Congress eliminated the Select Intelligence Oversight Panel in H.Res. 5. In March 2011, the chairman of the House Permanent Select Committee on Intelligence, Representative Mike Rogers, announced a plan to permit three members of the Appropriations Committee to participate in House Permanent Select Committee on Intelligence hearings and briefings. The goal of the initiative, according to Representative Rogers, was to "knit together the Intelligence Committee with the Appropriators and ... allow key appropriators important insights into the intelligence committee which they fund."[50] The proposal did not, however, change the responsibilities of the two committees.

Senate Initiatives

The Senate also recognized the need to respond to the 9/11 Commission's recommendations. In January 2004, the Senate adopted S.Res. 445 to improve the effectiveness of the Senate Select Committee on Intelligence and for other purposes. Section 402 of the resolution, which passed by a vote of 79-6-15, established a Subcommittee on Intelligence within the Senate Appropriations Committee "as soon as possible after the convening of the 109th Congress." S.Res. 445 did not, however, actually constitute a change to the Senate Rules, and the 109th Congress reshuffled appropriations subcommittees and jurisdictions without creating a subcommittee on intelligence.

In considering intelligence authorization in 2009, however, the Senate returned to the issue. The Intelligence Committee reported its version of FY2010 authorization legislation, S. 1494, which included a provision (Section 341) to express the sense of the Senate that a Subcommittee on Intelligence should be established within the Committee on Appropriations with the responsibility for approving an annual appropriations bill for the National Intelligence Program that would be considered by the full Appropriations Committee "without intervening review by any other subcommittee." The intelligence subcommittee would, however, automatically include the chairman and ranking Member of the Subcommittee on Defense. This provision was the subject of conversations between the chair of the Intelligence Committee and the ranking Member of the Appropriations Committee, and Section 341 was dropped from the bill before it passed the Senate by unanimous consent on September 16, 2009.[51] (The provision was not included in the final version of the FY2010 Intelligence Authorization Act, P.L. 111-259, that was eventually enacted in October 2010.)

During consideration of S.Res. 445 and on other occasions, it was argued that it would be difficult to create a subcommittee with a classified budget.[52] The actions taken by the Senate reflect the fact that classification has always been a key consideration in the congressional approach to intelligence appropriations. There has been little public discussion of the extent to which other factors relating to subcommittees' jurisdiction may have been important.

End Notes

[1] U.S. Congress, Senate Select Committee on Intelligence, "Current and Projected National Security Threats to the United States," March 12, 2013.

[2] 50 U.S.C. 401a(6).

[3] National Commission on Terrorist Attacks upon the United States, The 9/11 Commission Report, the Attack from Planning to Aftermath (New York: W.W. Norton, 2011), p. 416. For more information about these recommendations and congressional responses, see the appendix to this report.

[4] The Implementing the Recommendations of the 9/11 Commission Act of 2007 (P.L. 110-53), enacted August 3, 2007. The Office of the Director of National Intelligence, "DNI Releases Budget Figure for National Intelligence Program," press release, October 3, 2007. Intelligence Reform and Terrorism Prevention Act of 2004 (S. 2845, P.L. 108-458), enacted December 17, 2004.

[5] The Intelligence Authorization Act of 2010 (P.L. 111-259), enacted October 7, 2010.

[6] The U.S. Department of Defense, "DOD Releases Military Intelligence Program Top Line Budget for Fiscal 2007, 2008, 2009," March 11, 2011, available at http://www.defense.gov/releases/release.aspx?releaseid=14328.

[7] Constant dollars adjust for the effects of inflation and show real increases or decreases in purchasing power.

[8] The Office of the Director of National Intelligence, "DNI Releases FY2012 Appropriated Budget Figure for the National Intelligence Program," press release, October 30, 2012, available at http://www.dni.gov/index.php/newsroom/press-releases/96-press-releases-2012. The U.S. Department of Defense, "DOD Releases Military Intelligence Program Appropriated Top Line Budget for Fiscal 2012," press release, October 30, 2012, available at http://www.defense.gov/releases/release.aspx?releaseid=15648.

[9] The Office of the Director of National Intelligence, "DNI Releases Budget Figure for FY 2013 Appropriations Requested for the National Intelligence Program," press release, February 13, 2012, available at http://www.dni.gov/index.php/newsroom/press-releases/96-press-releases-2012/337-dni-releases-budget-figure-for-fy2013-appropriations-requested-for-the-national-intelligence-program. The U.S. Department of Defense, "DOD Releases Military Intelligence Program Requested Top Line Budget for Fiscal 2013," press release, February 13, 2012, available at http://www.defense.gov/releases/release.aspx?releaseid=15058l.

[10] DOD's budget justifications for Overseas Contingency Operations specify an amount requested for the MIP. They also include a "non-DOD classified" component that outside observers believe is a proxy for NIP OCO funding. For example, see page 6-5 of DOD's FY2013 budget request overview, available at http://comptroller.defense.gov/defbudget/fy2013/FY2013_Budget_Request_Overview_Book.pdf

[11] The Office of Senator Dianne Feinstein, "Senator Feinstein Vows to Cut Waste, Duplication from Intelligence Budget," press release, October 28, 2010. U.S. Congress, Senate Select Committee on Intelligence, Confirmation Hearing on the Nomination of James R. Clapper to be Director of National Intelligence, 111th Congress, 1st sess., July 20, 2010.

[12] This FY2001 figure is based on a 1995 House Appropriations Committee (HAC) disclosure, adjusted for inflation. The Committee indicated that the Administration's FY1995 NFIP request was for $16.3 billion. According to the Joint Inquiry into Intelligence Community Activities Before and After the Terrorist Attacks of September 11, 2001, p. 254, "As Chart 1.0 shows, the Intelligence Community budget fell or remained even in constant dollars throughout the 1990s." The chart referred to shows funding for the National Foreign Intelligence Program. The FY1995 figure is therefore a useful proxy for the NFIP budget in FY2001.

[13] DNI Clapper stated in testimony before the Senate Select Committee on Intelligence in March that sequestration would cut more than $4 billion from the NIP, bringing FY2013 intelligence spending to roughly $49 billion.

[14] In March 1998, DCI George Tenet announced that the FY1998 intelligence budget was $26.7 billion. The DCI statement referred to "aggregate amount appropriated for intelligence and intelligence-related activities." Using this of $26.7 billion figure as a baseline and adjusting for inflation provides an estimate of $37.38 billion in FY2001. For further analysis of the DCI statement, see footnote 16 below.

[15] Commission on the Roles and Capabilities of the U.S. Intelligence Community, Preparing for the 21st Century: An Appraisal of U.S. Intelligence, March 1, 1996. Since this report was published in 1996, the decline referred to here may have taken place between 1989 and 1995. The report discusses total intelligence funding—likely the NFIP as well as what was

then called Tactical Intelligence and Related Activities (TIARA). A third program, the Joint Military Intelligence Program (JMIP), was established by DOD in 1995. The JMIP and TIARA were subsequently combined to form the MIP.

[16] CRS requested but did not receive confirmation of these estimates from the Office of the DNI.

[17] The commission refers to "total intelligence (national, defense-wide, tactical) spending." The DCI statements refer to "aggregate amount appropriated for intelligence and intelligence-related activities." Of note, these DCI figures—$26.6 billion in nominal dollars for FY1997 and $26.7 billion in nominal dollars for FY1998—are close to figures disclosed by the House Appropriations Committee in 1994. According to HAC, the President's budget requested $16.3 billion for the NFIP and $10.4 billion for TIARA, for a total of $26.7 billion in nominal dollars for FY1995. This indicates (1) that the DCI's later disclosures are equivalent to national plus military intelligence and (2) that, in real terms assuming the amount appropriated for FY1995 was close to the amount requested, there was a slight decrease in total intelligence spending from FY1995 to FY1997.

[18] This analysis subtracts estimates for total intelligence spending from national defense spending—budget function 050—for each year since 1980. We use budget function 050, instead of budget function 051—Defense Department spending—because 050 includes defense-related spending for the Federal Bureau of Investigation and the Department of Homeland Security, along with spending for other members of the intelligence community, according to Office of Management and Budget materials.Those budget materials indicate 050 does not include funding for the Department of State and the Department of Treasury and therefore may not include funding for those department's intelligence community components. Nonetheless, the budgets for those intelligence community components are generally believed to be a very small portion of the national intelligence budget.

[19] U.S. Congress, Senate Select Committee on Intelligence, "Current and Projected National Security Threats to the United States," March 12, 2013.

[20] Richard Haass, Independent Task Force of the Council on Foreign Relations, Making Intelligence Smarter: The Future of U.S. Intelligence, 1996.

[21] Preparing for the 21st Century: An Appraisal of U.S. Intelligence, p. 79.

[22] U.S. Congress, House Permanent Select Committee on Intelligence, IC21: The Intelligence Community in the 21st Century, 104th Congress, 2nd Sess., June 5, 1996, p. 79.

[23] P.L. 102-496 previously granted the DCI the authority to "develop and present to the President the annual budget for the National Foreign Intelligence Program of the United States."

[24] Intelligence Community Directive 204, "Roles and Responsibilities for the National Intelligence Priorities Framework," September 13, 2007.

[25] Ibid.

[26] U.S. Congress, House Permanent Select Committee on Intelligence, Hearing on the Director of National Intelligence's 500-Day Plan, December 6, 2007.

[27] Intelligence Community Directive 116, "Intelligence Planning, Programming, Budgeting, and Evaluation System," September 14, 2011.

[28] Greg Miller, "Secret Report Raises Alarms on Intelligence Blind Spots because of AQ focus," The Washington Post, March 20, 2013.

[29] See for example Greg Miller, "Secret Report Raises Alarms on Intelligence Blind Spots Because of AQ focus," The Washington Post, March 20, 2013. According to the article, a classified report prepared by the President's Intelligence Advisory Board (PIAB) in 2012 allegedly found that, after a decade of counterterrorism and intelligence support to the wars in Iraq and Afghanistan, the CIA specifically and the intelligence community more generally has now become too focused on tactical operation and military. Some observers

believe the community has neglected its traditional functions of gathering and analyzing intelligence on more strategic topics. 30 50 U.S.C. 401a(6).

[31] See Dan Elkins, Managing Intelligence Resources, 3rd ed., (Dewy, AZ: DWE Press, 2010), pp. 4-16.

[32] 50 U.S.C. 403-1(c)(1).

[33] Reprogramming refers to the movement of NIP funds within an appropriations account. Transfer refers to the movement of NIP funds between a appropriations account.

[34] P.L. 108-458, The Intelligence Reform and Terrorism Prevention Act, § 1011.

[35] P.L. 112-74, § 8117. P.L. 113-6, § 8107

[36] 50 U.S.C. 403-1(c)(5)(A).

[37] P.L. 108-458, §1018.

[38] See, for instance, P.L. 111-118, the Department of Defense Appropriations Act, 2010. The CIA retirement fund received some $290 million; the ODNI received some $707; the two combined represented about one-fiftieth of the NIP.

[39] 9/11 Commission Report, p. 416.

[40] ODNI News Release No. 4-11, February 14, 2011.

[41] "Hearing of the Senate (Select) Intelligence Committee, Subject: Nomination of Lieutenant General James Clapper to be Director of National Intelligence," Federal News Service, July 20, 2010.

[42] In response to a question during a symposium on November 2, 2010, Director Clapper stated, "I've secured at least a conceptual agreement with the [S]ecretary of Defense to take the National Intelligence Program out of the Defense budget. And we plan to do—try to do that in 2013. I mention that because I think that's a—one specific way that we'll accrue more authority actually through ODNI, and the oversight and execution of that funding.... It's been $50 billion off the top line of the DOD. And it certainly gives, I think, ODNI a lot more authority and insight and transparency over that number." Office of the Director of National Intelligence, Remarks and Q & A by Director of National Intelligence Mr. James Clapper, 2010 Geospatial Intelligence Symposium, New Orleans, Louisiana, November 2, 2010.

[43] When asked, "Last year at [the Geoint Conference], you spoke about the importance of changing the budget structure and potentially putting the NIP in a separate category under the DNI. Can you give us a status update on that effort?" Clapper responded, "Ain't gonna happen." Office of the Director of National Intelligence, Remarks as delivered by Mr. James R. Clapper, Director of National Intelligence, GEOINT 2011 Symposium, October 17, 2011.

[44] Testimony of James R. Clapper, Jr. before the Senate Select Committee on Intelligence and House Permanent Select Committee on Intelligence, September 13, 2011, CQ Transcription.

[45] These limits can be enforced with a parliamentary point of order raised on the House or Senate floor. See CRS Report R42388, The Congressional Appropriations Process: An Introduction, by Jessica Tollestrup.

[46] Remarks and Q & A by Director of National Intelligence Mr. James Clapper, 2010 Geospatial Intelligence Symposium, New Orleans, Louisiana, November 2,2010.

[47] Remarks by Representative Obey, Congressional Record, January 9, 2007, p. H202.

[48] Remarks by Representative Dreier, Congressional Record, January 9, 2007, p. H201.

[49] Chairman Holt Statement, Panel Report to the Defense Subcommittee, Intelligence Activities in the FY 2009 Defense Appropriations Bill, July 11, 2008, reproduced at http://www.fas.org/irp/congress/2008_cr/holt071108.html.

[50] House of Representatives, Permanent Select Committee on Intelligence, Press Release, "Chairman Rogers Announces Strategic Partnership with House Appropriators," March 23, 2011.

[51] See remarks by Senator Feinstein, Congressional Record, September 16, 2009, p. S9447-S9448.

[52] See CRS Report RL33742, 9/11 Commission Recommendations: Implementation Status, and CRS Report RS21955, S.Res. 445: Senate Committee Reorganization for Homeland Security and Intelligence Matters.

In: Federal Intelligence Spending
Editor: Adaline Cortez

ISBN: 978-1-63117-037-9

Chapter 2

INTELLIGENCE, SURVEILLANCE, AND RECONNAISSANCE (ISR) ACQUISITION: ISSUES FOR CONGRESS*

Marshall Curtis Erwin

SUMMARY

Increasing calls for intelligence support and continuing innovations in intelligence technologies combine to create significant challenges for both the executive and legislative branches. Intelligence, surveillance, and reconnaissance (ISR) systems are integral components of both national policymaking and military operations, including counterterrorism operations, but they are costly and complicated and they must be linked in order to provide users with a comprehensive understanding of issues based on information from all sources. Relationships among organizations responsible for designing, acquiring, and operating these systems are also complicated, as are oversight arrangements in Congress. These complications have meant that even though many effective systems have been fielded, there have also been lengthy delays and massive cost overruns. Uncertainties about the long-term acquisition plans for ISR systems persist even as pressures continue

---

* This is an edited, reformatted and augmented version of a Congressional Research Service publication, CRS Report for Congress R41284, prepared for Members and Committees of Congress, from www.crs.gov, dated April 16, 2013.

for increasing the availability of ISR systems in current and future military operations and for national policymaking.

These challenges have been widely recognized. A number of independent assessments have urged development of "architectures" or roadmaps setting forth agreed-upon plans for requirements and acquisition and deployment schedules. Most observers would agree that such a document would be highly desirable, but there are significant reasons why developing such an architecture and gaining an enduring consensus remain problematic. First, ISR technologies are not static; whereas it is possible to plan for aircraft, ships, or tanks that can be used for decades, it is doubtful that today's inventory of satellites, unmanned aerial vehicles, and manned aircraft will still be the right mix a few years hence. Some believe that a "cast-in-concrete" plan would inhibit the ability to take advantage of new technologies or techniques as they emerge. Secondly, achieving consensus on such a plan would be greatly affected by the separate priorities of different parts of the intelligence community, the Defense Department, and Washington policymakers. The needs of policymakers and military commanders are different and are usually reconciled only on a case-by-case basis. Furthermore, different congressional oversight committees may also have different perspectives on priorities and some may seek to emphasize funding for specific systems.

The Director of National Intelligence could be given authority to reach across current organizational boundaries to define requirements and priorities. Some propose establishing a position for a separate "ISR Czar" to do this. Few observers believe that ISR programs could be carved out of the intelligence budget and/or the defense budget, and placed under the control of a single officer or lead agency. There is a strong likelihood that separate needs and concerns that affect the current systems will not disappear, even if one official has a new and expansive charter. Similar concerns would exist in regard to the jurisdictions of congressional oversight committees.

ISR issues will continue to be an area of concern for the 113th Congress, especially in light of the lack of a long-term investment strategy and the pending impact of sequestration. In testimony before the Senate Select Committee on Intelligence in March 2013, Director of National Intelligence James Clapper indicated that sequestration would delay major systems acquisition and require older reconnaissance systems to be decommissioned. The DNI and the President's FY2014 budget request indicated an effort to protect the intelligence community workforce, suggesting that hard choices in response to budget cuts will focus on ISR systems and other expensive collection platforms.

INTRODUCTION

Intelligence, surveillance, and reconnaissance (ISR) systems are matters of great congressional interest. These systems can provide policymakers with information on the military capabilities of foreign countries, the location of key defense and industrial sites, indications of the presence of weapons of mass destruction, and information on the plans of foreign leaders and terrorist groups. National-level ISR is essential for both defense planning and arms control negotiations. Military commanders rely on intelligence systems for information on enemy positions and activities; tactical ISR has also been essential for precise targeting in counterterrorism operations while minimizing civilian casualties. At present, major ISR systems—national and tactical—are used by both military commanders and Washington policymakers to follow developments in combat areas in great detail. ISR systems include reconnaissance satellites, some of which have been operational for decades; Unmanned Aerial Systems (UAS)[1] of various sizes; and manned aircraft and other sensor platforms. In practice, some ISR systems acquired for one purpose are regularly used for other missions that may have been unanticipated when the systems were designed.

Acquisition of ISR systems presents particular challenges to the intelligence community, the Department of Defense (DOD), and Congress. Agencies responsible for national systems are usually separate from those that design and acquire tactical systems. The costs and complexity of individual systems, continuing changes in technologies, and the difficulties involved in linking disparate systems together to serve a variety of consumers require different acquisition approaches than those often used for ships, tanks, and manned aircraft. Moreover, since the establishment of the United Launch Alliance in late 2006,[2] ISR satellites rely on launch platforms and other technologies used by non-intelligence satellites; thus, there is a necessity to coordinate intelligence satellite developments and launch schedules with elements of the national space effort that is managed by federal agencies outside DOD and the intelligence community.

UAS have demonstrated that on occasion they can provide data at a fraction of the costs of multibillion dollar satellites, but UAS acquisition efforts have been anything but simple. There has been a tendency to introduce new and untested capabilities to unmanned platforms, causing production delays and cost growth. Some policymakers would centralize UAS acquisition efforts under an executive agent (an initiative that Congress at one point mandated but then abandoned), but, in practice, the four services have been intent on acquiring different UAS that meet their perceived unique requirements. The result has often been excessive costs required for different systems with duplicative or overlapping capabilities. Other platforms for ISR collection, such as manned aircraft, continue to have important functions, but often they compete for agency funding with non-intelligence aircraft rather than with unmanned intelligence systems, and intelligence requirements may not receive the highest priorities. Acquisition efforts are further complicated by the fact that Congress addresses ISR programs through a number of committees, principally Armed Services, Intelligence, and Appropriations.

Such factors taken together have often led to piecemeal acquisition efforts, major cost overruns, and an inability to ensure that disparate systems can be linked effectively to yield a comprehensive intelligence picture. There have been production delays and only recently have UAS been available in adequate numbers to support the pace of operations in Iraq and Afghanistan. Observers argue—and a number of key Members of Congress have concurred—that the drawbacks inherent in past and current ISR acquisition efforts are serious enough to indicate that consideration should be given to the preparation of an agreed-upon multi-year plan or "architecture" that provides production schedules for currently planned ISR systems and the introduction of new platforms. If such a plan were agreed upon, advocates argue, it would be possible to restrain cost growth, ensure that all requirements had been considered, and establish the best possible mix of satellites and unmanned and manned systems. On the other hand, skeptics suggest that dynamic technologies and the changing international environment would nevertheless necessarily limit what can be done in terms of multi-year procurement efforts.

Evolving Requirements for ISR Systems

A key consideration underlying efforts to acquire, deploy, and operate ISR systems is the way or ways that they will be used. The need to gain insights into Soviet military capabilities during the Cold War provided the principal impetus for the sizable investments in global signals intelligence and overhead reconnaissance capabilities. These systems were considered "national," they were acquired primarily to support the President and key Cabinet members. A number of "national" organizations—especially the National Reconnaissance Office (NRO) and the National Security Agency (NSA), along with the Central Intelligence Agency (CIA) were established to gather and analyze information for senior policymakers. The ability of U.S. leaders to gauge the extent of Soviet strategic capabilities was essential to defense planning and arms control negotiations, but there was less capability to support military commanders in ongoing combat operations.

Beginning with Desert Shield in 1991, however, these national-level systems began to be adapted to tactical use in Iraq, Bosnia, Kosovo, Afghanistan, and elsewhere. Wherever U.S. forces have been deployed for combat there have been requirements for intensive intelligence support that called upon national systems that were not originally intended for tactical uses. In peacekeeping/peacemaking/stabilization operations, the overriding need to minimize attacks on civilians has led commanders and national-level leaders to seek ever more precise target data from all available sources of information.

In addition to adapting older systems to the demands of current modes of war fighting, newer ISR systems have also been employed with considerable success. In particular, UAS have proven their value as relatively low-cost systems that can be routinely used by ground commanders to acquire tactical intelligence. In regular use since the early 1990s, UAS range in size and sophistication from very small systems that can be launched by an individual soldier for short-range tactical operations to the high-altitude Global Hawk that can acquire much of the same information as reconnaissance satellites. The potential overlap, or possibility of close coordination between UAS and national satellites has, however, called into question the separate organizational and congressional oversight structures that have been established or have evolved over the past decades.

In spring 2009, Secretary of Defense Robert Gates argued in *Foreign Affairs* that the nature of U.S. strategic planning has unalterably changed. His comments summarize the evolution of defense and intelligence planning that guided the Administration's budget proposals for FY2010:

> [F]or far too long there was a belief or a hope that Iraq and Afghanistan were exotic distractions that would be wrapped up relatively soon—the regimes toppled, the insurgencies crushed, the troops brought home. Therefore we should not spend too much or buy too much equipment not already in our long-range procurement plans or turn our bureaucracies and processes upside down.... As a result of these failed assumptions, the capabilities most urgently needed by our warfighters, were for the most part fielded ad hoc and on the fly, developed outside the regular bureaucracy and funded in supplemental legislation that would go away when the wars did—if not sooner.
>
> ...

> [G]iven the types of situations the United States is likely to face ... the time has come to consider whether the specialized, often relatively low-tech equipment well suited for stability and counterinsurgency missions is also needed. It is time to think hard about how to institutionalize the procurement of such capabilities and get them fielded quickly.[3]

Secretary Gates was addressing issues of defense acquisition in general and not ISR systems in particular. It is clear, however, from the text of his speeches and his actions as Defense Secretary that he sees ISR support to warfighters as a major example of the challenge facing policymakers in both the executive branch and Congress. Military operations have increasingly come to depend upon the availability of copious amounts of real-time ISR. As a result of the commitment to Iraq and Afghanistan, requirements for ISR and the actual use of ISR data have grown exponentially in the past decade. The military priorities of both the Bush and Obama Administrations have established priorities for particular kinds of intelligence and thus particular types of intelligence collection systems.

The February 2010 Quadrennial Defense Review (QDR) Report reflected Secretary Gates's earlier statements:

> The wars we fighting today and assessments of the future security environment together demand that the United States retain and enhance a whole-of-government capability to succeed in large-scale counter-insurgency (COIN), stability, and counterterrorism (CT) operations in environments ranging from densely populated urban areas and mega-cities, to remote mountains, deserts, jungles, and littoral regions.
>
> Stability operations, large-scale counterinsurgency, and counter-terrorism operations are not niche challenges or the responsibility of a single Military Department, but rather require a portfolio of capabilities as well as sufficient capacity from across America's Armed Forces and other departments and agencies. Nor are these types of operations a transitory or anomalous phenomenon in the security landscape. On the contrary, we must expect that for the indefinite future, violent extremist groups, with or without state sponsorship, will continue to foment instability and challenge U.S. and allied interests.[4]

The QDR indicates that DOD has placed special emphasis on "certain capabilities that have been in consistently high demand and have proven to be key enablers of tactical and operational success."[5] These enablers include unmanned aircraft systems such as the MQ-1 Predator and MQ9 Reaper UAS[6] and manned aircraft systems such as the MC-12 Project Liberty aircraft.

ISR ACQUISITION PROCESSES

ISR systems are acquired in very different ways; the process is conducted in classified channels and there is no overall ISR package that is developed by the executive branch and forwarded to Congress for its consideration. Rather, different systems are treated separately and requests come to Congress in different ways. Funds are also authorized and appropriated in different legislative measures. As might be expected, the result can be disjointed, with duplicative coverage in some areas and shortfalls in others. The most important ISR category is the National Intelligence Program (NIP) that includes systems designed for the use of national policymakers—the President and the National Security Council (NSC). Other important ISR systems are designed for and operated by military commanders and are grouped in the Military Intelligence Program (MIP). However, NIP systems can also be used to support tactical operations, and MIP systems can collect information of interest to senior policymakers. Traditionally, satellites are acquired as part of the NIP, but some are now included in the MIP. Most UAS have been MIP systems as have manned aircraft in recent decades. The composition of annual NIP and MIP budget submissions are classified and available only to Members of Congress and appropriate committee staff.

"National" Space

The most expensive ISR system has been surveillance satellites, the development of which is perhaps the greatest accomplishment of U.S. intelligence. For many years the NRO—an agency created in 1961 with no public acknowledgement of its existence for over 30 years—was able to develop and acquire cutting edge reconnaissance systems. Early systems were placed into orbit only after many failures; costs were relatively unconstrained, and work proceeded in secret and with minimal oversight from either DOD or Congress. Reconnaissance satellites, in being able to delineate Soviet capabilities—and the absence thereof—made a major contribution to U.S. defense policies during the Cold War and, most observers would acknowledge, essentially justified their costs. The end of the Cold War reduced the need for satellite reconnaissance of foreign military forces; the "open-checkbook" approach to satellite acquisition ended. A reduction in intelligence budgets in the 1990s coincided with the beginning of the retirements of many in the generation of scientists and engineers that launched the satellite program.[7]

It is widely acknowledged that there is inherent tension between efforts to acquire new satellite technologies and the need to maintain and/or replace existing capabilities. Acquisition of systems using currently available technologies can yield stability and contained costs, while trying to push the technological envelope to acquire cutting-edge or "exquisite" systems can be more disruptive. In addition, the tendency to prefer large Cold War-era systems has drawbacks. A senior DOD official acknowledged:

> we have attempted to buy large monolithic systems that produce a capability that is one size fits all, i.e. a single system that satisfies all customers, without evaluating the full set of alternatives....
>
> This model is a Cold War relic, when space systems were needed to satisfy only the strategic policy decision maker and events unfolded in a fairly static timeline. Today's reality is that one size does not fit all.[8]

Further, the operational tempos in all of the Areas of Responsibility (AOR) diverge greatly and require different timeliness of access, volume, or fidelity. Developing a system that can satisfy all users all of the time is unsustainable, if not impossible.... deploying architectures with constellations of just a few satellites leave[s] the nation incredibly vulnerable and invites our adversaries to target our systems."[9]

Satellite acquisition is complicated. First, satellites overlap to some extent with airborne systems in terms of reconnaissance capabilities; there are potential trade-offs. Secondly, the acquisition and operations (especially the launching) of reconnaissance satellites is closely related to other types of satellites used for meteorology and communications that are not intelligence systems. As one report has noted:

> The U.S. space sector, in supporting commercial, scientific, and military applications of space, is embedded in our nation's economy, providing technological leadership and sustainment of the industrial base. To cite one leading example, the global Positioning System (GPS) is the world standard for precision navigation and timing, directly and indirectly affecting numerous aspects of everyday life. But other capabilities such as weather services; space-based data, telephone and video communications; and television broadcasts have also become common,

> routine services. The Space Foundation's 2008 Space Report indicates that the U.S. commercial satellite service and space infrastructure sector is today approximately a $170 billion annual business.[10]

Thus, the potential that high-altitude UAS have for meeting the same requirements as satellites may suggest that funds for satellite programs be shifted to UAS acquisition (leaving aside the issue of whether satellites actually provide better coverage and whether satellites are potentially less vulnerable to attack). On the other hand, if fewer reconnaissance satellites are to be launched, economies of scale among all satellite programs along with the "space intelligence base" might be affected.

Another program, the Space Based Infrared System (SBIRS) consisting of infrared sensors that can detect incoming missiles, demonstrates the cost risks inherent in satellite acquisition; according to one media account the program exceeded its original $3 billion cost estimate by some $7.5 billion. The SBIRS program, centered on a space-based missile warning satellite, "originally pegged at around $3 billion, is now in the neighborhood of $10 billion; launch of the first satellite, originally targeted for 2002, is now expected anywhere between late 2010 and spring 2011."[11]

Satellites have always been costly. In earlier decades their unique ability to peer behind the Iron Curtain justified substantial investments that were known only to a few members of relevant congressional committees. National satellites remain costly, reportedly over $1 billion for each satellite, not counting considerable associated ground support and analytical efforts. The effort to acquire new technologies or to exploit available cutting-edge technologies results in highly expensive systems. Many observers argue that costs of satellite systems are unnecessarily inflated by too great a commitment to innovative technologies when others are adequate for likely missions; others point to a tendency to add unnecessary requirements ("bells and whistles") that increase complexity and delay production. Others maintain that opportunities for technological breakthroughs should not be passed up and innovative technologies usually pay for themselves eventually. The growth of program costs, however, is beyond doubt.

Since passage of the Land Remote Sensing Policy Act of 1992 (P.L. 102-555), commercial imaging satellites have been launched, and federal agencies were the first major customers. Arguably, commercial imagery saves the government money since purchases can be limited to meet particular requirements. In large measure, however, imagery companies have become highly dependent on government contracts, and changes in imagery procurement can have great implications for the commercial industry. In many cases, government satellites can produce more detailed information but at higher costs, and the government has to cover both acquisition and operating costs over a multi-year period.

The end of the life-cycle for the current satellites was foreseen well ahead of time. Although plans for follow-on systems were and remain classified, there has been considerable public commentary about one approach, known as the Future Imagery Architecture (FIA), in which billions were invested only to have funding canceled in 2005 when it became apparent that delivery schedules and budget limitations could not be met. Most observers credit the FIA debacle as a result of choosing an inexperienced contractor, imposing excessively tight deadlines and cost controls without an adequate government oversight mechanism.[12]

In April 2009, Dennis Blair, newly appointed as DNI, announced a plan to modernize the satellite imagery architecture by having the NRO build and operate "satellites" (no number specified) and significantly increasing the acquisition of imagery produced by U.S. commercial providers. He noted that commercial "less-complex satellites, which are based on technologies already in production by U.S. vendors, would be available sooner than the much more capable NRO developed and acquired systems."[13] Media accounts indicate that efforts would be made to avoid the problems associated with FIA and that independent cost estimates and tougher assessments of technological maturity would be involved for the new systems that are due to operational before 2020.[14] Some Members, especially Senator Christopher Bond, the vice chairman of the Senate Intelligence Committee, have criticized the plan, arguing that there is an opportunity to take advantage of potential technological breakthroughs and proposing a different, but as yet untested, satellite technology.[15] The Administration proposal would provide a few highly sophisticated satellites that have the advantage of being based on available, proven technologies; Senator Bond's proposal, which was reportedly included in the FY2010 Intelligence Authorization bill, S. 1494, would include larger numbers of smaller, less expensive satellites that are based on cutting edge technologies that have not yet been tested and approved. Media accounts indicate that defense authorization (P.L. 111-84) and defense appropriations measures (P.L. 111-118) for FY2010 included funding for the acquisition of at least one of the larger satellites with funding beginning in FY2011.[16]

Several attempts have been made to provide overall direction to space surveillance acquisition efforts. In 2004 the National Security Space Office

(NSSO) was created to develop and coordinate national security space strategies, architectures, plans, programs, and processes on a continuing basis. The NSSO remains, however, essentially an advisory body and has not had the authority to define programs and monitor implementation. According to GAO the NSSO developed a National Security Space Strategy in 2004, but it was never issued.[17] In 2003 an Executive Agent for Space was established with the Secretary of the Air Force designated to fill the position.[18] The Executive Agent would have a wide range of responsibilities for planning and programming DOD's space systems, including Milestone Decision Authority. The persistence of space acquisition problems, however, led to the abandonment of the position in 2005 with procurement responsibilities returning to the office of the Assistant Secretary of Defense for Acquisition, Technology, and Logistics. In 2009, however, the Defense Appropriation Act, P.L. 111-118, provided $7 million for a Space and Intelligence Office (SIO) within the Office of the Under Secretary of Defense for Acquisition, Technology, and Logistics (USD(AT&L)). The new office is to serve as the DOD space architecture planning office; it is to provide a roadmap to Congress in mid-2010 on how it will be used in future space system architecture planning.

II. Tactical" Space

Although considerable efforts have been underway for many years to make information collected available for tactical use, collection priorities for NRO satellites are established by the DNI. Although military commanders may have the opportunity to request coverage of a given target, they cannot be certain that their requirements will be considered more important than those of other agencies. The inability of combatant commanders to obtain what they consider as adequate support from national satellite programs led to efforts for DOD to acquire satellites independently of the NRO for the primary support of the warfighters. Some saw significant advantages to be gained by moving beyond "the sclerotic national programs [that] simply cannot maintain the pace required for future operations."[19] The goal was to build new, less expensive, less sophisticated satellites that could meet the critical requirements of combat commanders. Under the program, known as Operationally Responsive Space (ORS), military commanders would have access to an inventory of relatively unsophisticated satellites that could be launched when needed to provide information for limited durations. ORS would complement information from national satellites and other collection programs.

Some observers have raised concerns that this program to some extent duplicates or at least overlaps the capabilities of NRO satellites and may have been established simply to avoid the organizational complexities of national satellite procurement and the need to coordinate collection management with Washington agencies.[20] The GAO concluded in 2008 that "the [ORS] concept is in the early stages of development and not commonly understood by all members of the warfighter and national security space communities." In addition "DOD has not clearly defined key elements of the ORS concept and has not effectively communicated the concept with key stakeholders." Furthermore, GAO believes that "officials from the intelligence community were concerned about DOD's lack of consultation and communication with them regarding the ORS concept." These officials "also raised concerns about the importance of using their current processes and architecture so as not to create unnecessary duplicative processes to get data to the war fighter."[21]

Other observers maintain, however, that new systems could be built from the bottom up using available technologies, including those used in the commercial sector, and that ORS could provide a useful capability for commanders, whose requirements will always be subject to adjustment or derogation when collection priorities of national systems are established and implemented.[22] ORS provides a just-in-time capability that can be tailored for missions of limited duration. The ORS concept has gained support in the Defense Department, and Congress has funded the ORS in defense authorization and appropriations legislation, albeit not to the extent envisioned by the Air Force. For FY2010 the Administration requested $112.9 million, an increase over the FY2009 appropriations level of $83.7 million, but over $100 million that was originally envisioned by ORS planners was included in an Air Force list of unfunded priorities.[23] The conference report reflected an agreement to provide only the $112 million requested, but not to provide the additional funds.[24] However, Defense officials believed that further ORS satellites will be approved if the first one can be built "within the kinds of very aggressive parameters that we've set up."[25] As the Administration requested only $93 million for the ORS program for FY2011, some observers suggest that the limited funds may ultimately jeopardize the program.[26] Nevertheless, support for ORS remains strong in both chambers; the House version of the FY2011 defense authorization bill (H.R. 5136) would add an additional $40 million to the Administration request and the Senate Armed Services Committee in its bill (S. 3454) would add an additional $20 million.

In April 2009, testimony of Josh Hartman, a long-time proponent of ORS, set for the rationale for what he termed "a balanced architecture":

> The solution is a change in our business model that will enable employment of an architecture distributed to multiple nodes and layered to provide right level of capability to the right geographic regions at the right times, while leveraging commercial systems and multiple sensors from different sizes of space craft and non-space platforms.
>
> This model would provide for a balanced architecture where a foundational capability would be provided from medium or large systems. At the same time, small and agile, less complex systems would be "layered" to augment in optimized orbits, with additional capability in high demand areas, and niche capability for special operations, irregular needs or crisis situations." As recommended by the GAO, evolution of capability would be a hallmark and key tenet of this model. Systems would be purposely be designed to live shorter lives to reduce the system complexity, synchronize on-orbit life with developing time, increase industry volume, and take advantage of rapidly advancing technology.[27]

In June 2011, the ORS-1 satellite was the first fully operational spacecraft to be launched as part of the ORS program and featured a modified SYERS-2 sensor, similar to the electro-optical and infrared imagery sensor used on the U-2 Dragon Lady aircraft.[28] On January 3, 2012, the ORS-1 satellite was declared operationally capable by General William Shelton, Air Force Space Command commander. The ORS system was launched 32 months after the idea was conceptualized, and combatant commanders accepted the asset less than 90 days after the launch.[29]

DOD is assessing other satellite systems besides ORS. Some hope to realize significant savings over NRO-led efforts. One media report suggests that one company believes it can deliver a halfmeter-resolution imagery satellite for $6 million-$7 million a satellite.[30] Efforts to take advantage of new technologies to produce relatively inexpensive satellites to support military commanders could usefully supplement intelligence gathered from other sources. At the same time, however, the ORS effort appears to have been undertaken in isolation from the organizations that have been responsible for launching satellites over many years. Observers suggest that the extensive expertise available in the NRO and NGA has not been fully accessed, possibly risking waste and duplication of effort. Alternately, some might argue that long-existing organizational relationships tend to become sclerotic, potentially inhibiting the development of innovative technologies that can serve operating forces at reasonable costs.

Unmanned Aerial Systems (UAS)

UAS have become essential parts of military operations.[31] Although first deployed during the Vietnam conflict, their use was limited until 1990-1991, when they supplied exact locating data during Operations Desert Storm that was used in targeting precision guided munitions (PGMs). Their use expanded during operations in Iraq and Afghanistan, when great emphasis has been placed on avoiding inadvertent attacks on civilians. Increasing availability of UAVs, especially the MQ-1 Predator with a range of 454 miles and the follow-on MQ-9 Reaper with a range of over 3,600 miles and a flight time of over 20 hours, has made them tactical weapons of choice. In addition to the Predators, longer-range Global Hawks, which fly at much higher altitudes, have also been employed in combat operations. Communications have improved to the point where information intercepted by UAVs can be forwarded not only to the local commander but also to intelligence centers at various echelons where it can be combined (or "fused") with data from other sources to produce a more complete intelligence picture.

The history of UAV acquisition has been complicated. A crucial step was taken during the Reagan Administration by Navy Secretary John Lehman, who, having witnessed Israeli use of the systems over Lebanon, procured commercially built Israeli UAVs for the U.S. Navy. Later, the Defense Airborne Reconnaissance Office (DARO) was established by DOD to manage UAV acquisition throughout the Defense Department; this effort did not, however, endure, and in the FY1998 Defense Authorization Act (P.L. 105-85, §905), Congress directed the transfer of relevant DARO functions to the separate military departments. Since then, some consideration has been given to designating one service as an executive agent for UAV acquisition, but this approach has never been accepted in the face of significant opposition from other services determined to ensure that their unique requirements can be met.

In recent years the use of UAVs has proliferated in Iraq and Afghanistan, where they helped in meeting the objectives of identifying elusive enemies and avoiding civilian casualties. According to DOD, "the number of deployed UAS has increased from approximately 167 aircraft in 2002 to over 6,000 in 2008, while defense investment in UAS capabilities has dramatically grown from $284 million in Fiscal Year 2000 to $2.5 billion in Fiscal Year 2008."[32]

The FY2011 request was for $4.1 billion. Responding to continuing needs for tactical systems, in the first months of the Obama Administration, Secretary of Defense Gates realigned DOD's budget priorities to emphasize tactical ISR systems including UAVs and manned ISR platforms. During this period, funding was recommended to field and sustain 50 continuous orbits for Predator or Reaper-class UAVs. In March 2012, Secretary of the Air Force Michael Donley, stated the requirement increased to 65 continuous orbits, with the ability to increase them to 85.[33] Manned ISR platforms such as the Air Force's MC-12W Project Liberty and the Army's various turbo-prop aircraft flown by Task Force ODIN, also shared this funding. Although additional funding for ISR systems was included in the FY2009 supplemental, Secretary Gates indicated his intention to ensure that ISR programs are incorporated into base budgets rather than in supplemental appropriations measures. He also indicated plans for more extensive research and development efforts on ISR systems with emphasis on those systems that link warfighters and national systems.[34]

The most commonly used UAV systems, Predators and Reapers, are designed for tactical use. The Predator flies at altitudes up to 25,000 feet; the Reaper 50,000 feet. Both have an endurance of 24 hours. Some UAVs, such as the Global Hawk, have capabilities that rival those of reconnaissance satellites. They can fly higher—over 60,000 feet—and longer—28 hours. There is potential overlap between Global Hawk capabilities and those of reconnaissance satellites. Development costs of UAS have tended to exceed initial estimates by significant amounts. Development costs of the Air Force's Global Hawks grew by 284%; the Reaper by 97%; the Shadow by 80%, and the Predator by 60%.[35] In some cases (especially with the Global Hawk) the increases resulted from immature technologies and fundamental restructurings; in others it was simply a matter of increasing the number of platforms to be acquired.

ISR acquisition requirements extend well beyond satellites and launch vehicles. The increasing use of large numbers of UAS and other mobile ISR systems requires different and more varied communications support. In particular, the commands using such tactical systems may not have access to major DOD communications networks based on fiberoptic cables and must instead rely on communications satellites. According to one assessment the latter are essential for "reach back" from tactical units to intelligence centers at higher echelons or in the United States, where the processing, exploitation, analysis, and dissemination of intelligence products occurs.[36] The increased use of tactical ISR systems increases requirements for the acquisition of communications satellites and for other systems to facilitate tactical communications with an increasing emphasis on Internet-based systems. As the study noted: "While small units may not require large quantities of ISR data, their needs are focused, immediate and critical when engaged with the enemy."[37]

UAS are procured by the four services, although efforts have been made to encourage shared use. An Air Force initiative in 2007 to be designated as executive agent for medium and high-altitude unmanned aerial vehicles was ultimately not approved, but efforts to make use of technologies developed for another service continue.

For instance, the Marine Corps determined that the Army's Shadow system could meet its requirements and by procuring an existing system saved the costs of development and obtained systems that could be rapidly be made available to the operating forces.[38]

Similarly, the Navy has taken advantage of various components of both Global Hawks and Reapers that were developed for the Air Force in acquiring its Broad Area Maritime Surveillance UAS.

Despite such initiatives GAO has argued that DOD should undertake a "rigorous and comprehensive analysis" of the requirements for UAS to identify commonalities and develop a strategy for making systems and subsystems more common and that the services should demonstrate that they have explored potentials for common platforms and sensors and are taking an "open systems approach" that will permit use of interchangeable sensors.[39] GAO further expressed concerns about cost growth in UAS programs, indicating that "development cost estimates for the 10 [UAV] programs we assessed, collectively, has increased more than $3.3 billion (37% in 2009 dollars) from initial estimates—with $2.7 billion attributed to the Air Force's Global Hawk program."[40]

The GAO underscored the advantages it believes can be gained by designing compatible unmanned systems that are effectively linked together especially using commercially available open sources.[41] On May 18, 2009, the Air Force announced its "Unmanned Aircraft Systems Flight Plan, 2009-2047."

The plan describes a family of UAS ranging from man-portable vehicles to larger, "tanker sized" platforms. The goal is to acquire "a common set of airframes within a family of systems with interoperable, modular 'plug and play' payloads, with standard interfaces."[42]

Manned Airborne Systems

The military services remain committed to the use of manned surveillance aircraft that can be configured for a variety of different missions depending upon specific requirements. Some systems still in use were originally designed for Cold War missions, but they continue to serve as platforms for use in tracking insurgents and improvised explosive devices. Eventually the older systems have to be retired; the Navy is currently acquiring over 100 P-8 Poseidon maritime surveillance aircraft to replace aging P-3s. The Air Force is considering P-8s as a possible replacement for the E-8 JSTARS aircraft, which has played a major role in supporting combat operations in Iraq and Afghanistan, although the E-8s are scheduled to have new engines to extend their service life. The P-8 is a modified Boeing 737-800 aircraft of proven reliability and can be fitted with various sensor systems depending on the particular mission. Its predecessor, the P-3, first entered service in the 1960s; P-8s are also expected to be available for decades. A recent media report indicated that the Army is even considering the development of intelligence-gathering airships.[43]

In comparison to the complex acquisition history of UAS, the process for acquiring manned aircraft, although not without challenges, generally follows well established procedures.

Congressional oversight in the House is shared between the Armed Services and Intelligence Committees and in the Senate is primarily the responsibility of the Armed Services Committee with input from the Intelligence Committee.

In April 2008, Secretary of Defense Gates established a Department of Defense-wide task force to identify and recommend solutions for increased ISR to the ground forces stationed in the U.S. Central Command area of responsibility. In his remarks to the Air Force's Air War College in Montgomery, AL, Defense Secretary Gates criticized the services for "not moving aggressively in wartime to provide resources needed now on the battlefield," and stated he had "been wrestling for months to get more intelligence, surveillance, and reconnaissance assets into the theatre." His direction was to find "more innovative and bold ways to help those whose lives are on the line" and stated the "deadlines for the task force's work are very short."[44]

The Air Force's response to the Secretary's demand was called "Project Liberty," a Beechcraft King Air 350 turbo-prop aircraft modified with an imagery and signals intelligence suite. To answer the Secretary's proposed timeline, the Air Force diverted from the well-established procedures of acquisition and purchased the first seven from the private sector, using COTS— "commercial off the shelf"—technology to convert the aircraft to an ISR platform.

By November 2008, the Air Force had signed a $171 million contract with Hawker Beechcraft Corporation, and four months later the first aircraft was delivered. In June 2009, the first MC-12 squadron at Balad Air Base, Iraq, flew the first combat mission. By December 2009, the entire MC-12 fleet was deemed operational.[45] Within 18 months, the Air Force fielded three expeditionary MC-12 squadrons and the associated processing, exploitation, and dissemination entities to both Iraq and Afghanistan.[46]

Project Liberty was considered the fastest delivery of an Air Force weapons system from "concept to combat" since the P-51 Mustang in World War II.[47] The MC-12 is now considered the most heavily tasked manned airframe in the combat Air Force.

ASSESSMENTS OF ISR ACQUISITION PROCESSES

ISR acquisition efforts, given their size and cost, have generated significant public controversy, but public discussions are hampered by the absence of relevant information that is unclassified. However, there have been a number of recent outside reviews conducted by properly cleared outsiders. In general, these assessments have faulted organizational arrangements for the acquisition of ISR systems. A 2008 study conducted by the congressionally chartered *Independent Assessment Panel on the Organization and Management of National Security Space* (sometimes described as the Allard Commission after a key congressional sponsor, former Senator Wayne Allard) described the current organization for space systems used for national (as opposed to tactical) purposes:

"Authorities and responsibilities are spread across numerous organizations, including many within the Office of the Secretary of Defense (OSD) [Under Secretary of Defense (USD/Intelligence], USD/Acquisition, Technology and Logistics; USD/Policy; and the Assistant Secretary of Defense (ASD/Networks & Integration], USAF, USN, USA, USMC, DARPA [Defense Advanced Research Projects Agency], MDA [Missile Defense Agency], and NRO. Furthermore:

- There is no standing forum or mechanism below the level of the President to coordinate efforts among the agencies responsible for NSS or to adjudicate differences over requirements and resources.
  - The predominant capability providers are NRO and SMC [Space and Missile Systems Center, a component of the Air Force's Space Command], which today have parallel requirements and funding paths within the IC and DOD.
  - Space capability providers in NOAA [National Oceanic and Atmospheric Administration], NASA [National Aeronautics and Space Administration], and other federal agencies have their own requirements, funding, and reporting chains.
- Within DOD, there is no common authority below the Secretary of Defense to integrate space acquisition programs and resources, or to adjudicate differences
  - There are separate requirements and funding chains within the Pentagon for the Air Force, NRO, DARPA, MDA [Missile Defense Agency], Navy and Army, commercial satellite communications, and commercial imagery.
- A structure for coordinating space operations between DOD and the intelligence community is emerging and is thought to be on target."[48]

The Independent Assessment Panel argued that the President should establish and execute a National Space Strategy and establish a National Security Space Authority who would be jointly responsible to the Secretary of Defense and to the DNI and charged with defining the space budget for DOD and the intelligence community and executing the program with milestone decision authority. There would also be an effort to improve the qualifications of Air Force and NRO acquisition professionals. Most controversially, the panel would create a National Security Space Organization, which would combine several Air Force space offices with the NRO under the National Security Space Authority. Arguably, this official might be perceived as a security space "czar" with a role subordinate to one Cabinet officer and the DNI.[49]

In 2008 the *House Permanent Select Committee on Intelligence (HPSCI)* undertook its own assessment of U.S. space capabilities. The resulting report reflected the conclusions of the committee's majority, that the United States is "losing its preeminence in space." The report focused on the need for an "integrated overhead roadmap" or "architecture." By "architecture," HPSCI meant

- a problem-driven approach that is based on securing prioritized, well-defined national security interests;
- a comprehensive solution that balances the financial investment against the overall risk to national security;
- a realistic delivery schedule that meets the defined timeline that in many cases must be flexible and updated against the risk; and
- a plan to migrate from a requirements-based acquisition approach towards a capabilities-based strategy, with the proviso that a purely capabilities-based approach could introduce additional challenges.[50]

Although the report acknowledged that executive branch officials believed they had provided a plan, committee members disagreed, maintaining that "there is no comprehensive space architecture or strategic plan that accommodates current and future national security priorities, DOD and intelligence community capability requirements."[51] The committee suggested that the practice has been for requirements to be added during the acquisition process resulting in added costs and delays and the need to resolve repeatedly the differing priorities of DOD and the intelligence community. When cutting-edge—and not yet available—technologies are chosen, the committee suggests that uncertainty and need for further testing complicate acquisition.

The report alluded to the interest of some to develop space systems solely for operational commanders in isolation from the NRO. Presumably reference was being made to the ORS; HPSCI suggested that "it is not in the best interest of the country to pursue separate national and military space architectures."[52] The House report recommended that R&D be treated as a national security priority and protected against from diversion to immediate operational needs.[53]

The HPSCI report raised concerns about programs jointly funded in the National Intelligence Program (NIP) and the Military Intelligence Program (MIP). The NIP is designed to provide intelligence systems that can supply information primarily of interest to national-level policymakers; the MIP supports combatant commanders. Although there is pervasive overlap between the two sets of systems, there is also concern that, in some instances, funds from the NIP have in effect been used by DOD to fund what are essentially MIP projects.

The committee report also addressed use of commercial imagery and statutes and regulations governing space commerce. Members of the committee's minority criticized several aspects of the report and maintained that it failed to "address the importance of integrated ground systems for tasking, processing, exploitation and dissemination."[54]

In November 2008 a *Joint Defense Science Board and Intelligence Science Board* task force on integrating sensor-collected intelligence produced a report looking at various flaws in current ISR efforts that extend beyond acquisition issues. It argued that ISR efforts can be better improved by integrating data from multiple sensors rather than by improving the design and performance of single sensors. In making this argument the task force pointed to structural issues that complicate such data integration. To accomplish this goal the task force recommended ensuring the inclusion of meta-data (or tags that describe specific data that can in turn be searchable whereas the data itself may not be) that can allow identification of information of specific interest. The task force's emphasis on better ways to access and analyze data is influenced by the vast expansion in data available and in many cases never exploited. It tended to favor a larger number of less sophisticated systems and achieve increased performance by integrating data from multiple sensors and platforms.[55]

Significant problems derive from limitations on the dissemination of collected data. Currently, meta-data are not consistently applied and tags are not consistent from agency to agency. Military commanders demand much larger quantities and more sophisticated types of intelligence (especially tactical imagery), but in many cases are unaware of and incapable of accessing data available throughout the intelligence community. "The number of images and signal intercepts are well beyond the capacity of the existing analyst community so there are huge backlogs for translators and image interpreters and much of the collected data are never reviewed. Further, decision makers and intelligence analyst have difficulty knowing what information is available."[56] Although an enormous number of full-motion video missions in support of tactical commanders have been conducted in Iraq and Afghanistan, the task force suggested that surveillance has often been episodic and continuing coverage of a given region had not always been possible.

The task force report emphasized that the ISR concept encompasses more than platforms for collection. It noted that DOD has developed the Global Information Grid, which includes a high-speed communications network of various ground, air, and space components. There is a need, according to the task force, for better ways for tactical commanders to access this information "on the move," and thus it emphasized the advantages of assured and accessible communications as would be made available by the redundant and complementary communications capabilities— terrestrial fiber, government and civilian communications satellites, networks built and maintained by specific agencies. (The task force advocated the Transformational Satellite System (TSAT) to provide links to the fiber network to mobile and fixed theater commands. TSAT was subsequently killed by DOD because it was considered duplicative.) A key goal should be, according to the task force, to ensure that future communications systems adhere to interoperability standards to ensure that they can support joint and international operations as well as "reach back" to U.S. agencies for analytical support. The essential concern of the task force was to ensure that the ongoing proliferation of platforms and sensors be matched by sufficient communications capabilities to enable their use. Currently, they found that "Our rapidly growing airborne ISR collection capabilities are not in balance with supporting communications."[57]

Furthermore, the task force noted that even though the Office of the Under Secretary of Defense for Intelligence (USDI) is double-hatted as Director of Defense Intelligence under the DNI, his judgment on space programs is affected by decisions of the Under Secretary of Defense for Acquisition, Technology, and Logistics (AT&L), whose mandate encompasses all DOD programs and is not limited to intelligence programs.

The report reflected a concern that DOD requirements, including to some extent tactical ISR requirements, are being met at the cost of supporting national needs, echoing HPSCI's concerns. The task force found that there is a perception that intelligence officials may not be empowered to balance national and tactical requirements. The report noted the decline in the number of trained and experienced government program managers who are able to conduct extensive acquisition initiatives over a multi-year period. The report criticized short tours of duty for acquisitions personnel that precluded the development of deep expertise in specific systems and over-reliance on advisory contractors. The lack of expertise was criticized as contributing to delays and costly changes in specifications. More broadly, the report noted declining numbers of students pursuing engineering degrees and a reluctance of some to seek careers in the satellite area, where work can be repetitive and sporadic. The tendency in recent years to focus on satellites that can fulfill current missions may discourage students who are most interested in "cutting-edge" R&D.

The *Government Accountability Office (GAO)* has assessed ongoing space systems acquisitions issues over a number of years. In a May 2009 report it recommended that a formal space plan based on a national security space strategy is essential for managing the acquisition and deployment of space systems. Without a strategy (and a plan to implement it) "the defense and intelligence communities may continue to make independent decisions and use resources that are not necessarily based on national priorities, which could lead to gaps in some areas of space operations and redundancies in others."[58]

In March 2009 GAO testified to the Senate Armed Services Committee in regard to challenges facing DOD in space acquisitions. Echoing the views of other assessments, GAO found

- on a broad scale, DOD starts more weapon programs than it can afford, creating a competition for funding that encourages low cost estimating, optimistic scheduling, overpromising, suppressing bad news, and, for space programs, forsaking the opportunity to identify and assess potentially more executable alternatives;
- DOD has tended to start its space programs too early, that is, before it has the assurance that the capabilities it is pursuing can be achieved within available resources and time constraints—in part a result of the tendency to favor acquisition programs over efforts to ensure that new technologies are reliable;
- DOD has tended to prefer fewer but heavier, larger, and more complex satellites than larger constellations of smaller satellites;
- several more recent space programs began in the late 1990s, when contracts were restructured in ways that reduced government oversight and shifted decision-making responsibilities to contractors, a situation that magnified problems relating to requirements creep and poor contractor performance.[59]

GAO generally recommended a number of best practices of the commercial sector to separate technology discovery from acquisition, follow incremental paths to meet user needs, match resources and requirements at program's start, and use quantifiable data and demonstrable knowledge to decide when to move to a new program phase. GAO acknowledged that DOD was attempting to implement some of these practices and noted legislative initiatives that were later enacted.[60] GAO also went further to underscore the difficulties resulting from the fact that requirements, resource allocation, and acquisition processes are led by different organizations and the need to strengthen coordination of military and intelligence space efforts. As noted above, GAO has been skeptical of the Operationally Responsive Space effort due to its separation from other intelligence space programs even though it envisions smaller satellites built with available, proven technologies.

In January 2010 GAO forwarded another report to the Subcommittee on Air and Land forces of the House Committee on Armed Services that expressed concern about the ability of the services to share information within combat theaters.[61] GAO recommended that DOD establish a concept of operations to provide direction and priorities for sharing intelligence information across the defense intelligence community. GAO also urged the services to develop their own implementation plans and set timelines for sharing data with the rest of DOD.

THE OBAMA ADMINISTRATION'S APPROACH

Although outlines of the Obama Administration's overall approach to longer-term ISR acquisition issues have not been publicly detailed, the Administration has taken an initial approach based on acquiring additional reconnaissance platforms that are based on currently available technologies. In April 2008, Defense Secretary Gates, having been frustrated by reports from the field regarding inadequate numbers of UAVs, established an ISR Task Force that eventually made a number of recommendations to maximize the availability of systems in the inventory and to acquire adequate numbers of additional systems.[62]

Based on these findings, in April 2009, Secretary Gates forwarded the Administration's plans for ISR programs in the FY2010 budget based on his determination to "to rebalance this department's programs in order to institutionalize and enhance our capabilities to fight the wars we are in and the scenarios we are most likely to face in the years ahead, while at the same time providing a hedge against other risks and contingencies."[63]

"First, we will increase intelligence, surveillance and reconnaissance (ISR) support for the warfighter in the base budget by some $2 billion. This will include

- Fielding and sustaining 65 continuous RPA orbits with the ability to increase them to 85 and maximizing their production.[64] This capability, which has been in such high demand in both Iraq and Afghanistan, will not be permanently funded in the base budget. It will represent a 62% increase in capability over the current level and 127% from over a year ago.

- Increasing manned ISR capabilities such as the turbo-prop aircraft deployed so successfully as part of 'Task Force Odin' in Iraq.
- Maintaining the Air Force's MC-12 Project Liberty aircraft.
- Initiating research and development on a number of ISR enhancements and experimental platforms optimized for today's battlefield."[65]

The Administration proposal apparently does not include efforts to acquire "exquisite" satellite technologies that are at best still in the research and development stage. Congress essentially endorsed this approach in FY2010 defense appropriations and authorization legislation (P.L. 111- 118 and P.L. 111-84).

Media reports indicate that the Obama Administration ordered a thorough review of existing national space policy, including national intelligence assets, originally intended for completion by October 2009, but which has not been made public.[66]

In May 2009 Defense Secretary Gates indicated that he and the DNI had agreed that a new charter for the National Reconnaissance Office (NRO) is needed given that the original one is decades old. A committee headed by retired Air Force General Trey Obering was asked to look at the NRO's roles and missions, and reportedly recommended that the NRO structure should not be altered. In March 2010 the DNI and the Secretary of Defense endorsed a set of organizing principles for the NRO that is intended to serve as a foundation for a revised NRO charter.[67]

On September 21, 2010, the Director of National Intelligence Jim Clapper and Secretary of Defense Bill Gates officially signed the newest NRO charter, also referred to as a memorandum of agreement. The first signed since 1965, this agreement formalizes the role of the NRO Director as responsible for managing and operating NRO programs, serving as the principal advisor on overhead systems to the Secretary of Defense and the DNI. The new charter also grants direct access to the NRO Director to both the Defense Secretary and the DNI.[68]

Information on the ISR component of the Administration's FY2011 budget request is mostly classified, but DOD did state that an additional $2.6 billion was added for contingency operations in Afghanistan and Iraq at the recommendation of DOD's ISR Task Force, including nearly doubling procurement of the MQ-9 Reapers.[69] ISR funding requested for ongoing combat operations rose from \$5.9 billion in FY2010 to \$7.0 in FY2011.

Congressional Initiatives

Congressional oversight of the acquisition of surveillance systems has its own challenges. ISR systems are overseen by the armed services, intelligence, and appropriations committees. Most aspects of the ISR program are necessarily secret. Historically, the "national" systems were overseen by the intelligence committees, whereas the tactical systems were usually overseen by the armed services committees (although the House Intelligence Committee had jurisdiction over both tactical and national systems). Public statements by some Members indicate, however, that important differences among committees exist in regard to current plans for satellite programs, and there have been considerable differences in regard to UAS programs, as well. There is widespread frustration about cost growth of ISR systems, unnecessary duplication of effort, and the possibility of inadequate collection.

A significant factor has been the absence of intelligence authorization legislation for over five years. This suggests that the congressional role has been primarily exercised by the appropriations and armed services committees. Some observers believe that these committees may tend to focus on ISR systems as components of larger defense programs whereas the intelligence committees might have focused more on support to national policymakers.

In addition to authorizing and appropriating funds for specific ISR systems, Congress has repeatedly emphasized the need for a more comprehensive approach to ISR as a whole. The October 2008 report by the House Permanent Select Committee on Intelligence noted that "members of Congress have repeatedly expressed their disappointment that no architectural plan exists, and have repeatedly asked the Administration for the plan. The lack of an integrated architecture was one of the first issues to face the DNI after the office was established in 2005. The frustration has continued to this day, and many believe that the nation is no closer to having a clearly defined plan than it was three years ago."[70] The HPSCI majority recommended that the years. The report is to include estimated levels of annual funding to carry out the programs.[74] The bill, H.R. 3326, was eventually enacted as P.L. 111-118; it mandated that DOD deliver a 15-Year Space System Investment Strategy by May 2010.

There are indications that ORS funding issues have led to broader questions about efforts to use space platforms to support national security goals. In its October 2008 report on the need for a space architecture, the House Intelligence Committee recommended that DOD and the DNI "develop a common architecture for all space-related systems" and urged that "[o]rganizations proposing new satellites should demonstrate how their proposals fit into the architecture."[75] In May 2009 the Senate Appropriations Committee reported the defense appropriations act for FY2010 with an expression of concern that

> the committee is concerned about the tendency of temporary, single-issue acquisition initiatives to grow into persistent, stovepiped bureaucracies with increasingly ambiguous mandates. This tendency is often the result of deficiencies in the acquisitions process, in which urgent joint requirements are too often not effectively addressed.[76]

Section 911 of the FY2011 Defense Authorization bill, P.L. 111-383, signed by the President on January 7, 2011, requires that the Secretary of Defense and the DNI "shall develop an integrated process for national security space architecture planning, development, coordination, and analysis." The effort is to include both defense and intelligence efforts, to provide mid-term to long-term recommendations to guide acquisitions, and is independent of but coordinated with efforts by the military departments and intelligence agencies. The accompanying report to an earlier version of the legislation (H.R. 5136) by the House Armed Services Committee indicates a determination to provide a clear mandate to conduct integrated space architecture planning in order to avoid isolated, stove-piped, efforts by the services and intelligence agencies. The committee added, nevertheless, that, "This section would not be intended to limit rapid acquisition efforts such as Operationally Responsive Space (ORS); however, the committee does endorse efforts that expand user access to ORS capabilities and data."[77]

The various reviews requested are likely to be forward in classified channels and it is not known if summaries will be publicly available. Nor is it known how consistent the studies will be with budgetary requests, but they will clearly provide benchmarks for Congress as consideration of annual legislation proceeds.

The 112th Congress

Congress continues to indicate concern about ISR issues, especially those relating to expensive space systems. The House version of the FY2012 defense appropriations bill, H.R. 2219, included a provision (§8089) that would mandate the establishment of a major program category for space in future defense programs. The accompanying report noted:

> Over the past decade, various attempts for alternative systems have been suggested and in some cases funded. Several of those attempts included the parallel development of alternative systems or technologies. These systems were advertised as being less expensive, more capable, and less risky. In each case, these alternative systems were terminated due to cost or complexity.[78]

Although the requirement for making space a major program category was not included in the enacted version, H.R. 2055, the conference report, H .Rept. 112-331, indicated congressional approval of block buys of satellites that evolved from previous designs (as opposed to reliance on wholly new technologies). The conferees also noted disappointment that it took DOD over two years to develop a 15-year space strategic plan. The report directed that the next 15-year plan be delivered with the FY2014 budget submission.[79]

Concern about the possibility of a sequestration of defense spending arose at the end of 2011 with the inability of the Joint Select Committee on Deficit Reduction to reach an agreement. In November 2011 Secretary of Defense Leon Panetta indicated in a letter to Senators John McCain and Lindsey Graham the longer-term effects of sequestration could include the delay or termination of major space initiatives, including space protection, communications satellites, and ISR systems.[80]

Most recently, both the Senate and House reports accompanying their respective FY2013 National Defense Authorization Acts indicated continued congressional concern about the lack of a strategy guiding ISR acquisition. The House directed DOD's Joint Requirements Oversight Council to conduct a strategic review of current, planned, and programmed ISR capabilities. [81] The Senate report similarly noted.

> "The [armed services] committee is aware of the increased demand for persistent intelligence, surveillance, and reconnaissance (ISR) resources to meet each combatant command's full range of military

operations. The committee acknowledges the Department of Defense has had to make difficult decisions on the acquisition, procurement, and allocation of its persistent ISR assets due to fiscal constraints alone. However, Congress has not been provided a formal report outlining the Department of Defense's long-term investment strategy to develop, procure, and sustain the necessary ISR platforms to meet these ISR collection requirements.[82]

The 113th Congress

ISR issues will continue to be an area of concern, especially in light of the lack of a long-term investment strategy called for by the 112th Congress and the pending impact of sequestration. In testimony before the Senate Select Committee on Intelligence in March 2013, Director of National Intelligence James Clapper indicated that sequestration would delay major systems acquisition and require older reconnaissance systems to be decommissioned. The President's FY2014 budget request noted that the intelligence community was responding to new budget realities by terminating or reducing programs that are a lower priority and cited as an example "an initiative to transition to a more efficient space-based architecture." The DNI and the FY2014 budget request indicated an effort to protect the intelligence community workforce, suggesting that hard choices in response to budget cuts will focus on ISR systems and other expensive collection platforms.

CONCLUSION

Many consider the desirability of a long-range plan or architecture for the deployment of surveillance assets is a given, but suspect it is almost unobtainable. Future intelligence requirements may change from those recently indicated by Secretary Gates. The policies and military capabilities of sophisticated nation states may again become the highest collection priorities of the intelligence community, rather than terrorist groups that are currently the chief concern. Similarly, there are no indications that technological capabilities of ISR systems have reached a stabile plateau, and basing future plans on current technologies may prove to be shortsighted. There are inherent challenges involved in establishing plans for acquisitions over a multi-year span, even if they are arguably outweighed by the limitations of annual planning cycles.

Ultimately, most recognize that there are limitations on what Congress can do to shape the international environment or the emergence of new technologies. Congress can, however, alter the roles and missions of the organizations involved in ISR programs acquisition, as well as authorize and appropriate funds for ISR systems acquisition. Some observers have suggested a number of steps internal to Congress that might improve the acquisition process for ISR systems. The 9/11 Commission, for instance, recommended that the intelligence committees be provided with responsibilities for both authorization and appropriations.[83] Others have recommended a separate annual intelligence appropriations act and subcommittees for intelligence within the two appropriations committees. Such initiatives would allow greater concentration on intelligence programs as separate and distinct from defense programs. On the other hand, such separation could complicate the close linkages and desirable duplication between some intelligence and defense programs. Congress could also set up special panels to look at ISR programs with representatives from current intelligence, armed services, homeland security, and appropriations committees.

Nevertheless, many of the complications involving ISR systems derive from the organization of the executive branch and current policies. The ability of the ODNI and DOD (including both the USD(I) or the USD (AT&L)) to establish an agreed-upon acquisition plan is inevitably a key factor. The role of the staffs of the National Security Council and the Office of Management and Budget in overseeing and monitoring acquisition plans and their implementation is also important.

Some observers conclude that, ultimately, there must be some form of an overhead surveillance architecture, even if it cannot be set "in concrete" for a multi-year period. In this view, it must include not only the collection platforms, but also associated communications, and data processing and analysis systems. In ongoing legislative dialogue, the executive and legislative branches will be challenged to design and fund systems that maximize adaptability to new missions while accepting reasonable cost constraints. Such a goal will require not only careful interagency and inter-branch coordination, but also a willingness by all involved to accept decisions that do not fully meet the goals of each and every agency. Observers suggest a key role for congressional committees in minimizing the role of initiatives launched by "special interests" that ultimately could add significant unnecessary costs, and do not deliver maximum collection contributions. The unique perspectives of the armed services, intelligence, and appropriations committees, if considered together, arguably could provide the comprehensive oversight that has occasionally eluded the executive branch.

ISR has revolutionized military operations in the past half-century; it is today an essential component of national security planning and operations. At the same time, experience shows that not all the billions of dollars that have been invested have resulted in useful systems. Acquiring and using ISR systems is likely to remain a substantial challenge for the U.S. government in coming decades and one that will depend on effective cooperation among the intelligence community, the Defense Department, and Congress.

End Notes

[1] According to the Defense Department, Unmanned Aerial Systems (UAS) refer to systems whose components include the necessary equipment, network, and personnel to control an unmanned aircraft. An Unmanned Aerial Vehicle (UAV) refers to a powered aerial vehicle that does not carry a human operation, uses aerodynamic forces to provide vehicle life, can fly autonomously or be piloted remotely, can be expendable or recoverable, and can carry a lethal or nonlethal payload. Thus UAS is a broader term that includes equipment, networks, and personnel in addition to the UAV; in practice the terms UAS and UAV are often used interchangeably. See Department of Defense, Dictionary of Military and Associated Terms, Joint Publication 1-02, 12 April 2001, updated through April 2010.

[2] See http://www.ulalaunch.com for information on the cooperative effort by Lockheed Martin and Boeing to provide space launch services to federal agencies.

[3] Robert M. Gates, "A Balanced Strategy: Reprogramming the Pentagon for a New Age," Foreign Affairs, January/February 2009, pp. 34-35.

[4] U.S. Department of Defense, Quadrennial Defense Review Report, February 2010, p. 20.

[5] Ibid., p. 21.

[6] Ibid., p. 22. It is noteworthy that the QDR does not specifically address satellite surveillance systems although it makes reference to the fact that "[f]orces in Iraq, Afghanistan, and elsewhere have developed new and more effective means for rapidly processing, exploiting, and fusing information from a wide array of sources and disseminating this information to operators at the tactical level," pp. 22-23. The "wide array" undoubtedly includes national satellite systems.

[7] See Joshua Boehm and Craig Baker, "A History of United States National Security Space Management and Organization," Prepared for the Commission to Assess United States National Security Space Management and Organization [2001].

[8] Testimony of Josh Hartman, Senior Advisor to the Under Secretary of Defense (Acquisition, Technology & Logistics) before the House of Representatives, Committee on Armed Services, Subcommittee on Strategic Forces, April 30, 2009.

[9] Ibid.

[10] Institute for Defense Analyses, Leadership, Management, and Organization for National Security Space: Report to Congress of the Independent Assessment Panel on the Organization and Management of National Security Space, July 2008, p. 2.

[11] Turner Brinton, "Software Fix Adds $750M to SBIRS Price Tag," Space News, July 27, 2009, p. A3.

[12] See Philip Taubman, "In Death of Spy Satellite Program, Lofty Plans and Unrealistic Bids," New York Times, November 11, 2007.

[13] Office of the Director of National Intelligence, "DNI Blair Announces Plan for the Next Generation of ElectroOptical Satellites," ODNI News Release No. 12-09, April 7, 2009.

[14] Andrea Shalal-Esa, U.S. Plans New Government Owned Satellites," Washington Post, April 8, 2009.

[15] See Tim Starks, "Senate Intelligence Bill Would Conflict With Wishes of Obama, Other Panels," CQ Today, July 14, 2009. Earlier, some observers concluded that differences over satellite acquisitions had doomed efforts to pass an intelligence authorization bill for FY2009. See Tim Starks, "Did a Satellite Dispute Knock Intelligence Bill From Orbit? Congressional Quarterly, March 31, 2009.

[16] See Warren Ferster, "Lawmakers Near Agreement on White House Spy Satellite Plan," Space News, October 19, 2009.

[17] See Davi M. D'Agostino, Director, Defense Capabilities and Management, Government Accountability Office to the Hon. Bill Nelson and the Hon. Jeff Sessions, Subcommittee on Strategic Forces, Committee on Armed Services., Defense Space Activities: National Security Space Strategy Needed to Guide Future DOD Space Efforts, GAO-08- 431R, March 27, 2008, p. 10.

[18] Department of Defense Directive 5101.2 of June 3, 2003.

[19] Arthur K. Cebrowski and John W. Raymond, "Operationally Responsive Space: A New Defense Business Model," Parameters, Summer 2005, p. 70.

[20] See Turner Brinton, "ORS Office's Success May Hinge on Its Ability to Skirt the Bureaucracy," Space News, May 11, 2009, p. A6.

[21] Ibid., p. 18; U.S. Government Accountability Office, Defense Space Activities: DOD Needs to Further Clarify the Operationally Responsive Space Concept and Plan to Integrate and Support Future Satellites, GAO-08-831, June 2008, p. 4.

[22] See GAO-08-831.

[23] Letter from Norton A. Schwartz, General, USAF, Chief of Staff to the Hon. John M. McHugh, May 18, 2009, available at http://www.afa.org/grl/pdfs/AirForceFY10 Unfunded RequirementsList.pdf.

[24] U.S. Congress, 111th Congress, 1st session, House of Representatives, Committee of Conference, National Defense Authorization Act for Fiscal Year 2010, October 7, 2009, H.Rept. 111-288, p. 1015.

[25] Testimony of General C. Robert Kehler, Commander, Air Force Space Command, before the Strategic Forces Subcommittee of the House Armed Services Committee, May 21, 2009.

[26] See John T. Bennett, "USAF Surprised OSD by Putting Small Sats on Wish List," Defense News, June 8, 2009, p.6. For additional background on Air Force funding priorities, see James B. Armor, Jr., The Air Force's Other Blind Spot, Space Review, September 15, 2008.

[27] Statement of Josh Hartman, Special Advisor to the Under Secretary of Defense (Acquisition, Technology and Logistics) to the House Armed Services Committee, April 30, 2009.

[28] See Michael P. Kleiman, "Operationally Responsive Space-1 satellite declared mission ready," available at http://www.kirtland.af.mil/news/story.asp?id=123287795, January 27, 2012.

[29] See William Graham, "Orbital Minotaur I launches with ORS-1 following eventful count," available at http://www.nasaspaceflight.com/2011/06/live-orbital-minotaur-i-launch-ors-1, June 29, 2011.

[30] Turner Brinton, "Uncertainty Looms Office Amid Declining Budget Projections for 3-year-old ORS," Space News, April 23, 2010.

[31] UAS, especially the larger platforms such as the Global Hawk, can also have "national" missions.

[32] Department of Defense, Quadrennial Roles and Missions Review Report, January 2009, p. 25.

[33] Speech by Michael Donley, Secretary of the Air Force, "Air Force Reserve: Integral to the Total Force," remarks at 2012 Air Force Reserve Senior Leader Conference, March 26-27, also available at http://www.af.mil/information/speeches/speech.asp?id=702, March 26, 2012.

[34] U.S., Department of Defense, Defense Budget Recommendation Statement, April 6, 2009.

[35] See U.S. Government Accountability Office, Defense Acquisitions: Opportunities Exist to Achieve Greater Commonality and Efficiencies among Unmanned Aircraft Systems, GAO-09-520, July 2009, p. 8.

[36] See U.S. Department of Defense, Office of the Under Secretary of Defense for Acquisition, Technology, and Logistics, Report of the Joint Defense Science Board/Intelligence Science Board Task Force, Integrating Sensor-Collected Intelligence, November 2008, p. 86.

[37] Ibid., p. 89; the report strongly recommended the Joint Tactical Radio System and the Transformational Satellite System.

[38] GAO-09-520, p. 3.

[39] Ibid., p. 4.

[40] Ibid., p. 2. It is noteworthy, however, that per unit costs for the widely deployed Predator have actually declined by 41%; see p. 10.

[41] The limitations of commercial systems were, however, revealed when reports surfaced that enemy fighters were downloading unencrypted information from Predator communications links; see Pauline Jelinek, "Pentagon: Insurgents Intercepted Drone Spy Videos," Washington Post, December 18, 2009.

[42] U.S. Air Force, United States Air Force Unmanned Aircraft Systems Flight Plan, 2009-2047, May 2009.

[43] Walter Pincus, "Military Seeks an Intelligence-Gathering Airship," Washington Post, February 16, 2010, p. A11.

[44] Speech of Secretary William Gates, Secretary of Defense, before the U.S. Air Force War College, Maxwell-Gunter Air Force Base, Ala., April 21, 2008. Available at http://www.defense.gov/speeches/speech.aspx?speechid=1231.

[45] Due to the record setting acquisition, training, and deployment timeline, Air Force officials nominated the MC-12W Project Liberty team for the Collier Trophy, an elite aviation recognition.

[46] See Renni Thornton, "MC-12 begins mission in southern Afghanistan," available at http://www.acc.af.mil/news/ story.asp?id=123198971, April 8, 2010.

[47] See Russell Petcoff, "Final MC-12 deployed to USCENTCOM AOR," available at http://www.af.mil/news/ story.asp?id=123213117, July 12, 2010.

[48] Institute for Defense Analyses, Leadership, Management, and Organization for National Security Space: Report to Congress of the Independent Assessment Panel on the Organization and Management of National Security Space, July 2008, pp. ES-4, 14. Senator Allard endorsed most of these recommendations in a floor speech in which he indicated the need for "a top-to-bottom overhaul to restore the vitality of our space programs." Congressional Record, November 19, 2008, pp. S10636-10637. Similar conclusions were also reached by the Committee for U.S. Space Leadership, a group of industry leaders; see

Turner Brinton, "Nonpartisan Group Urges Obama to Tackle Systemic Space Problems," Space News, February 23, 2009, p. 6.

[49] See testimony of Secretary of Defense Gates, Hearing of the House Armed Services Committee, May 13, 2009, Federal New Service Transcript.

[50] U.S. Congress, House Permanent Select Committee on Intelligence, Report on Challenges and Recommendations for United States Overhead Architecture, 110th Cong., 2nd sess., October 3, 2008, H.Rept. 110-914 (Washington: GPO, 2008), p. 8.

[51] Ibid., p. 2.

[52] Ibid., p 9.

[53] Ibid., p 14.

[54] Ibid., p. 27.

[55] U.S. Department of Defense, Office of the Under Secretary of Defense for Acquisition, Technology, and Logistics, Report of the Joint Defense Science Board/Intelligence Science Board Task Force, Integrating Sensor-Collected Intelligence, November 2008, p. 63.

[56] Ibid., p. 65.

[57] Ibid, p. 26.

[58] U.S. Government Accountability Office, Defense Space Activities: National Security Space Strategy Needed to Guide Future DOD Space Efforts, GAO-08-431R, March 27, 2008. See also GAO, Space Acquisitions: DOD Needs a Departmentwide Strategy for Pursuing Low-Cost, Responsive Tactical Space Capabilities, GAO-06-449, March 2006.

[59] U.S. Government Accountability Office, Space Acquisitions: DOD Faces Substantial Challenges in Developing New Space Systems, GAO-09-705T, May 20, 2009, pp. 8-9. The last point has also been made by Scott F. Large, the Director of the NRO, "National Security Space Collaboration as a National Defense Imperative," High Frontier, August 2008, p. 4.

[60] These initiatives included P.L. 111-23, the Weapons Systems Acquisition Reform Act of 2009.

[61] U.S. Government Accountability Office, Intelligence, Surveillance, and Reconnaissance: Establishing Guidance, Timelines, and Accountability for Integrating Intelligence Data Would Improve Information Sharing, GAO-10-265NI, January 2010. In May 2010 the House Armed Services Committee endorsed GAO's recommendations and asked for a report from DOD indicating implementation plans. U.S. Congress, 111th Congress, 2d session, House of Representatives, Committee on Armed Services, National Defense Authorization Act for Fiscal Year 2011, H.Rept. 111-491, May 21, 2010, p. 339-340.

[62] The ISR Task Force was not designed to be permanent but a congressional requirement was established (in S.Rept. 111-20) for DOD to report on the strategy chosen to transition its responsibilities by October 1, 2009. This deadline was apparently not met. (See explanatory statement accompanying the Defense Appropriations Act, Congressional Record, December 16, 2009, p. H15043.)

[63] Robert M. Gates, Defense Budget Recommendation Statement (Arlington, VA), April 6, 2009.

[64] Speech by Michael Donley, Secretary of the Air Force, "Air Force Reserve: Integral to the Total Force," remarks at 2012 Air Force Reserve Senior Leader Conference, March 26-27, also available at http://www.af.mil/information/ speeches/speech.asp?id=702, March 26, 2012.

[65] Ibid. For background to Gates decision making, see Greg Jaffe, "A Single-Minded focus on Dual Wars," Washington Post, May 15, 2009.

[66] Amy Klamper, "President Orders Sweeping U.S. Space Policy Review," Space News, July 6, 2009, p. 6.

[67] Statement for the Record, Betty Sapp, Principal Deputy Director, National Reconnaissance Office, before the House Armed Services Committee, Subcommittee on Strategic Services, April 21, 2010.

[68] See Dr. Bruce Berkowitz, "The National Reconnaissance Office at 50 Years: A Brief History," Center for the Study of National Reconnaissance, also available at http://www.nro.gov/history/csnr/programs/NRO_Brief_History.pdf, September 2011.

[69] Department of Defense, Overview—FY 2011 Defense Budget, March 2010, pp. 4-2.

[70] Challenges and Recommendations for United States Overhead Architecture, H.Rept. 110-914, p. 8.

[71] Ibid., p. 9.

[72] U.S. Department of Defense, DOD News Briefing with Undersecretary Flournoy and Vice Adm. Stanley, February 1, 2010.

[73] Congressional Record, December 16, 2009, p. H15043.

[74] U.S. Congress, 111th Congress, 1st session, House Committee on Appropriations, Department of Defense Appropriations Bill, 2010, to accompany H.R. 3326, July 24, 2009, H.Rept. 111-230, pp. 278-279.

[75] Ibid., p. 3.

[76] U.S. Congress, 111th congress, 1st session, Senate Committee on Appropriations, Making Supplemental Appropriations for the Fiscal Year Ending September 30, 2009, and for Other Purposes, Report to accompany S. 1054, S .Rept. 111-20, May 14, 2009, p. 15.

[77] U.S. Congress, 111th Congress, 2d session, House of Representatives, Committee on Armed Services, National Defense Authorization Act for Fiscal Year 2011, H.Rept. 111-491, May 21, 2010, p. 342-343.

[78] U.S. Congress, 112th Congress, 1st session, House of Representatives, Department of Defense Appropriations Bill, 2012, H .Rept. 112-110, June 16, 2011, p. 185.

[79] U.S. Congress, 112th Congress, 1st session, Committee of Conference, Military Construction and Veterans Affairs and Related Agencies Appropriations Act, 2012, H .Rept. 112-331, December 15, 2011, p. 657.

[80] http://defensenews.com/projects/pdfs/mccain-graham-letter.pdf.

[81] U.S. Congress, 112th Congress, 2nd session, House of Representatives, National Defense Authorization Act of 2013, H .Rept. 112-479, May 11, 2012.

[82] U.S. Congress, 112th Congress, 2nd session, Senate, National Defense Authorization Act for Fiscal Year 2013, S.Rept. 112-173, June 4, 2012.

[83] National Commission on Terrorist Attacks Upon the United States, Final Report, Washington: GPO, 2004, p. 420.

In: Federal Intelligence Spending
Editor: Adaline Cortez

ISBN: 978-1-63117-037-9

Chapter 3

INTELLIGENCE ISSUES FOR CONGRESS*

Marshall Curtis Erwin

SUMMARY

To address the challenges facing the U.S. intelligence community in the 21st century, congressional and executive branch initiatives have sought to improve coordination among the different agencies and to encourage better analysis. In December 2004, the Intelligence Reform and Terrorism Prevention Act (P.L. 108-458) was signed, providing for a Director of National Intelligence (DNI) with authorities to manage the national intelligence effort. The legislation also established a Director of the Central Intelligence Agency (CIA).

Making cooperation effective presents substantial leadership and managerial challenges. The needs of diverse intelligence "consumers" must all be met, using many of the same systems and personnel. The DNI has substantial statutory authorities to address these issues, but the organizational relationships remain complex, especially for intelligence agencies that are part of the Defense Department. Members of Congress in their oversight role may seek to observe the extent to which effective coordination is accomplished.

The intelligence community, which comprises 17 agencies, has experienced a decade of budgetary growth. That era was typified by (1) institution building with embryonic organization such as the Office of the

---

* This is an edited, reformatted and augmented version of a Congressional Research Service publication, CRS Report for Congress RL33539, prepared for Members and Committees of Congress, from www.crs.gov, dated April 23, 2013.

DNI and other new or evolving intelligence components, (2) information sharing and collaboration across those institutions, and (3) a focus on counterterrorism.

While those issues will remain areas of congressional interest, Members will likely confronted by a new set of intelligence challenges resulting from budgetary realities and from second-order effects stemming from post-9/11 changes. These include:

- Consolidation and redundancy. Intelligence collection systems are expensive and some critics suggest there have been elements of waste and unneeded duplication of effort. The Administration is considering long-term reductions with an emphasis on potentially redundant information technology systems. There is great concern, however, that any reductions be carefully made to avoid curtailing capabilities that have become integral to military operations and to policymaking in many areas.
- Information security and management. The WikiLeaks disclosures that began in 2010 and other recent incidents of unauthorized disclosure of classified information have drawn considerable attention to the risks that widespread information sharing entails. Investigations into the 2009 Christmas day bombing attempt and the Fort Hood shooting also suggest analysts are now challenged to synthesize the large volumes of information being shared.
- Intelligence support to counterterrorism and operations. The Administration's targeting killing program raises legal, jurisdictional, and efficacy issues. Broader questions have also been raised about whether intelligence agencies have become too focused on counterterrorism to the detriment of other national security priorities and whether some of those functions should be transitioned to U.S. military control, allowing intelligence agencies to focus on traditional collection and analysis.

Most Recent Developments

Intelligence officials and Members of Congress are addressing ways to reduce intelligence spending while protecting core capabilities. Director of National Intelligence (DNI) James R. Clapper Jr. recently stated that sequestration would require a 7% cut, or roughly $4 billion, to the National Intelligence Program (NIP) budget and warned of reduced global coverage and decreased human and technical intelligence collection. Mr. Clapper also warned of repercussions similar to those that occurred in the 1990s when the intelligence community saw a 23% cut in its budget, resulting in a "damaging downward spiral."[1] Those cuts allegedly distorted the intelligence workforce, resulting in what is sometimes referred to as a "bathtub" shaped employment curve, with large numbers of older employees and new hires but few mid-level professionals capable of steering the community through post-9/11 changes.

Congress completed action on the FY2013 intelligence authorization legislation (S. 3454) in December 2012. The Senate passed its version of the bill by voice vote on December 28. The House approved the Senate version by a 373-29-29 vote on December 31. The final bill was signed into law by the President on January 14, 2013 (P.L. 112-277). The bill reflected funding above the President's request but below the $53.9 billion appropriated for FY2012.

BACKGROUND AND ANALYSIS

The attacks on the World Trade Center and the Pentagon on September 11, 2001, dramatically demonstrated the intelligence threats facing the United States in the new century. In response, Congress approved significantly larger intelligence budgets and, in December 2004, passed the most extensive reorganization of the intelligence community since the National Security Act of 1947. The Intelligence Reform and Terrorism Prevention Act of 2004 (hereinafter, the "Intelligence Reform Act") (P.L. 108-458) created a Director of National Intelligence (separate from a Director of the Central Intelligence Agency) who heads the intelligence community, serves as the principal intelligence adviser to the President, and oversees and directs the acquisition of major collections systems. As long urged by some outside observers, one individual is now charged with concentrating on the intelligence community as a whole and possesses statutory authorities for establishing priorities for budgets, for directing collection by the whole range of technical systems and human agents, and for the preparation of community-wide analytical products.

P.L. 108-458 was designed to address the findings of the National Commission on Terrorist Attacks Upon the United States, known as the 9/11 Commission, that there has been inadequate coordination of the national intelligence effort and that the intelligence community, as then organized, could not serve as an agile information gathering network in the struggle against international terrorists. The commission released its report in late July 2004, and Congress debated its recommendations through the following months. A key issue was the extent of the authorities of the DNI, especially with regard to management and budgeting for technical collection systems managed by Defense Department agencies. In the end, many of the recommendations of the 9/11 Commission regarding intelligence organization were adopted after a compromise provision was included that called for implementing the act "in a manner that respects and does not abrogate" the statutory authorities of department heads.

For additional information about intelligence community reform, background on intelligence collection disciplines, and intelligence budgeting, please see *Appendix A* to this report. The text below provides a brief overview of the intelligence community and of enduring intelligence oversight issues and then discusses specific topics that may be addressed by the 113th Congress.

Intelligence Community

The intelligence community (defined at 50 U.S.C. 401a(4)) consists of the following:

The Office of the Director of National Intelligence
Central Intelligence Agency (CIA)
Bureau of Intelligence and Research, Department of State (INR)
Defense Intelligence Agency (DIA)
National Security Agency (NSA)
National Reconnaissance Office (NRO)
National Geospatial-Intelligence Agency (NGA)
The National Security Branch, Federal Bureau of Investigation (FBI)
Army Intelligence
Navy Intelligence
Air Force Intelligence
Marine Corps Intelligence
Coast Guard Intelligence
The Office of Intelligence and Analysis, Department of the Treasury
The Office of Intelligence, Department of Energy
The Office of National Security Intelligence, Drug Enforcement Administration (DEA)
The Office of Intelligence and Analysis, Department of Homeland Security

Except for the CIA, intelligence offices or agencies are components of Cabinet departments with other roles and missions. The intelligence offices/agencies, however, participate in intelligence community activities while supporting the other efforts of their departments.

The CIA remains the keystone of the analytic efforts of the intelligence community. It has all-source analytical capabilities that cover the whole world outside U.S. borders. It produces a range of studies that address virtually any topic of interest to national security policymakers. The CIA also collects intelligence with human sources and, on occasion, undertakes covert actions at the direction of the President. (A covert action is an activity or activities of the U.S. government to influence political, economic, or military conditions abroad, where it is intended that the U.S. role will not be apparent or acknowledged publicly.)

Three major national-level intelligence agencies in the Department of Defense (DOD)—the National Security Agency (NSA), the National Reconnaissance Office (NRO), and the National Geospatial-Intelligence Agency (NGA)—absorb the larger part of the national intelligence budget. NSA is responsible for signals intelligence and has collection sites throughout the world. The NRO develops and operates reconnaissance satellites. The NGA prepares the geospatial data—ranging from maps and charts to sophisticated computerized databases—necessary for humanitarian operations and for targeting in an era in which military operations are dependent upon precision-guided weapons. In addition to these three agencies, the Defense Intelligence Agency (DIA) is responsible for defense attachés and for providing DOD with a variety of analytical products. It serves as the premier all-source analytic unit within DOD. Although the Intelligence Reform Act provides extensive budgetary and management authorities over these agencies to the DNI, it does not revoke the responsibilities of the Secretary of Defense for these agencies.

The State Department's Bureau of Intelligence and Research (INR) is one of the smaller components of the intelligence community but is widely recognized for the high quality of its analysis. INR is strictly an analytical agency; diplomatic reporting from embassies, though highly useful to intelligence analysts, is not considered an intelligence function (nor is it budgeted as one).

The key intelligence functions of the FBI relate to counterterrorism and counterintelligence. The former mission has grown enormously in importance since September 2001, many new analysts have been hired, and the FBI has been reorganized in an attempt to ensure that intelligence functions are not subordinated to traditional law enforcement efforts. Most importantly, law enforcement information, including counterterrorism and counterintelligence information, is now expected to be forwarded to other intelligence agencies for use in all-source products.

The intelligence organizations of the four military services concentrate largely on concerns related to their specific missions. Their analytical products, along with those of DIA, supplement the work of CIA analysts and provide greater depth on key military and technical issues.

The Homeland Security Act (P.L. 107-296) provided the new Department of Homeland Security (DHS) responsibilities for fusing law enforcement and intelligence information relating to terrorist threats to the homeland. The Office of Intelligence and Analysis in DHS participates in the inter-agency counterterrorism efforts and, along with the FBI, has focused on ensuring that state and local law enforcement officials receive information on terrorist threats from national-level intelligence agencies.

The Coast Guard, now part of the DHS, deals with information relating to maritime security and homeland defense. The Energy Department analyzes foreign nuclear weapons programs as well as nuclear nonproliferation and energy-security issues. It also has a robust counterintelligence effort. The Treasury Department collects and processes information that may affect U.S. fiscal and monetary policies. Treasury also covers the terrorist financing issue.

Authorization Legislation

Annual intelligence authorization bills were enacted from FY1979 through FY2005, providing congressional authorization for intelligence programs and guidance to the several intelligence agencies in specific provisions and report language. No intelligence authorization legislation was enacted between December 2004 and October 2010.

Annual intelligence authorization acts were first passed in 1978 after the establishment of the two congressional intelligence committees. These acts provided specific authorizations of intelligence activities and were accompanied by reports that provided detailed guidance to the nation's intelligence agencies. The absence of intelligence authorization acts meant that key intelligence issues were addressed in defense authorization acts and defense appropriations acts that focused primarily on the activities of the Department of Defense. Several Members have maintained that this procedure resulted in misplaced priorities and wasteful spending estimates that could run into billions.

However, over the last two years, Congress has met its statutory requirement by passing three Intelligence Authorization bills (for FY2011, FY2012, and FY2013) that included classified schedules of authorizations and that were signed into law. Most recently, in December 2012, both the House and Senate passed S. 3454, the Intelligence Authorization for FY2013, which was signed into law by the President on January 14, 2013 (P.L. 112-277). Key issues debated during the passage of these bills included the adequacy of Director of National Intelligence (DNI) authorities, Government Accountability Office (GAO) audit authority over the Intelligence Community, and measures to combat national security leaks. These three bills appear to reflect a determination to underscore the continuing need for specific annual intelligence authorization legislation.

ENDURING OVERSIGHT ISSUES

Duplication of Effort

The Intelligence Reform and Terrorism Prevention Act of 2004 tasks the DNI with ensuring the elimination of waste and unnecessary duplication within the intelligence community. Some observers believe the DNI has focused more on other statutory requirements—specifically its mandate to facilitate information sharing—while neglecting this responsibility to eliminate waste, resulting in the proliferation of intelligence organizations, particularly in the areas of counterterrorism and analysis, that fulfill many of the same functions.

Redundancy can serve important functions in intelligence. In the more tactical venues like counterterrorism, having multiple foreign and domestic intelligence organizations working to identify and disrupt terror plots ensures due diligence on the large amount of threat reporting flowing into the intelligence community each day. For example, in the wake of the 2009 Christmas day attack, a White House review noted that, "As with intentional analytic redundancy, the counterterrorism community also has multiple and overlapping warning systems to ensure that departments and agencies are kept fully aware of ongoing threat streams."[2] In the area of strategic analysis, redundancy might more effectively check the biases of individual organizations. The DNI commented on this issue in July 2010, noting, "'Competitive analysis' avoids single points of failure and unchallenged analytic judgments. The lack of competing analytic judgments was a criticism by several post-9/11 commissions."[3] Notionally, such competition might have improved the pre-war analysis of Iraq's weapons of mass destruction capacity.

Striking a balance that eliminates unnecessary redundancy while maintaining the competitive environment that has proven effective over the last decade at preventing at least large-scale, 9/11- type attacks will likely be the greatest challenge facing the 113th Congress in the area of intelligence.

Information Sharing vs. Information Overload

Investigations of the 9/11 attacks concluded that both technical and policy barriers had limited sharing of information collected by different agencies that, if viewed together, could have provided forewarning into the unfolding plot. This insight led to a series of reforms. The USA Patriot Act eliminated statutory barriers to information sharing, primarily in the domestic intelligence arena, and the Intelligence Reform and Terrorism Prevention Act of 2004 created the broader institutional framework for sharing across the intelligence community. That 2004 act gave the DNI the authority to "ensure maximum availability of and access to intelligence information within the intelligence community." Intelligence successes and failures in recent years suggest significant improvement has been made in the area of information sharing. A White House review of the 2009 Christmas day bombing attempt, for example, found that "Information sharing does not appear to have contributed to this intelligence failure," and that information about a pending attack had been shared with those in a position to disrupt the plot.[4] A Senate investigation into the 2012 attack on the diplomatic mission in Benghazi, Libya, similarly concluded that intelligence was effectively shared between the Department of State and other intelligence agencies prior to the incident. John Brennan, in a prehearing question for his confirmation hearing as CIA Director, stated his view that sharing between the intelligence community, DOD, and other intelligence and law enforcement partners was at an all-time high.[5]

While the intelligence community is not entirely without its legacy "stovepipes,"[6] the challenge more than a decade after 9/11 is largely one of information overload, not information sharing. Analysts now face the task of connecting disparate, minute data points buried within large volumes of intelligence traffic shared between different intelligence agencies. According to a DNI statement from July 2010, "Terabytes of foreign intelligence information come in each day, vastly exceeding the entire text holdings of the Library of Congress, which is estimated at 10 terabytes." In the additional views section of the Senate report on the Christmas day bombing attempt, Senators Saxby Chambliss and Richard Burr noted that analysts who could have connected the dots prior to the incident struggled to search the large volume of terrorism-related intelligence available to them.[7] The same problem was identified at the FBI in the aftermath of the 2009 Foot Hood shooting.[8]

While not a new problem for the intelligence community, the challenge of "separating the wheat from the chaff" may have been exacerbated over the last decade by a number of factors, including the fusion of domestic and foreign intelligence and the use of new information technologies that generate large amounts of data accessible to the federal government. Congress may wish to revisit the technical and institutional changes implemented by the intelligence community since this problem came into focus in 2009.[9]

Counterterrorism and Intelligence Support to Military Forces

In 1997, the House Intelligence Committee noted that "intelligence is now incorporated into the very fiber of tactical military operational activities, whether forces are being utilized to conduct humanitarian missions or are engaged in full-scale combat." The Persian Gulf War demonstrated the importance of intelligence from both tactical and national systems, including satellites that had been previously directed almost entirely at Soviet facilities. There were, nonetheless, numerous technical difficulties, especially in transmitting data in usable formats and in a timely manner. Many of these issues have since been addressed with congressional support and in Operation Iraqi Freedom intelligence was an integral part of the operational campaign and remained so in both Iraq and Afghanistan.

A classified report prepared by the President's Intelligence Advisory Board (PIAB) in 2012 allegedly found that, after a decade of counterterrorism and intelligence support to the wars in Iraq and Afghanistan, the CIA specifically and the intelligence community more generally has now become too focused on tactical operation and military.[10] Some observers believe the community has neglected its traditional functions of gathering and analyzing intelligence on more strategic topics. Members expressed similar concerns during recent confirmation hearings for CIA Director Brennan, who signaled his intent to examine allocation of mission within the CIA.[11]

The DNI is responsible for establishing intelligence community priorities and has a staff dedicated to ensuring collection and analytic resources are properly allocated to meet those priorities. In light of these mechanisms, the findings of the PIAB might be overstated. Some argue that an alleged focus on counterterrorism and operational support may reflect public perception of intelligence community activity rather than an actual allocation of intelligence resources.[12]

Collection Capabilities

Intelligence agencies collect vast quantities of information on a daily, even an hourly, basis. The ability to locate fixed installations and moving targets has become an integral component of U.S. military capabilities. On almost any subject, the intelligence community can provide a wealth of knowledge within short time frames. Inevitably, there are "mysteries" that remain unknowable—the effects of unforeseeable developments and the intentions of foreign leaders. The emergence of the international terrorist threat has posed major challenges to intelligence agencies largely designed to gather information about nation states and their armed forces. Sophisticated terrorist groups in some cases relay information only via agents in order to avoid having their communications intercepted. Human collection has been widely perceived as inadequate, especially in regard to terrorism; the Intelligence Reform Act stated the sense of Congress that, while human intelligence (humint) officers have performed admirably and honorably, there must be an increased emphasis on and greater resources applied to enhancing the depth and breadth of human intelligence capabilities. In October 2005 the National Clandestine Service was established at CIA to manage humint operations by CIA and coordinate humint efforts by other intelligence agencies.

There are also congressional concerns regarding major technical systems—especially reconnaissance satellites. These programs have substantial budgetary implications. Whereas the intelligence community was a major technological innovator during the Cold War, today both intelligence agencies and their potential targets make extensive use of commercial technologies, including sophisticated encryption systems. Consensus has yet to be reached on acquisition programs for a new generation of satellites.

Analytical Quality

The ultimate goal of intelligence is to provide accurate analysis in a timely manner. Analysis is not, however, an exact science and there have been, and undoubtedly will continue to be, failures by analysts to prepare accurate and timely assessments and estimates. The performance of the intelligence community's analytical offices during the past decade is a matter of debate; some argue that overall the quality of analysis has been high while others point to the failure to provide advance warning of the 9/11 attacks and a flawed estimate of Iraqi weapons of mass destruction as reflecting systemic problems. Congressional intelligence committees have for some time noted weaknesses in analysis, a lack of language skills, and a predominant focus on current intelligence at the expense of strategic analysis.

Analytical shortcomings are not readily addressed by legislation, but Congress has increased funding for analytical offices since 9/11 and the Intelligence Reform Act of 2004 contains a number of provisions designed to improve analysis—an institutionalized mechanism for alternate or "red team" analyses to be undertaken (§1017), the designation of an individual or entity to ensure that intelligence products are timely, objective, and independent of political considerations (§1019), and the designation of an official in the office of the DNI to whom analysts can turn for counsel, arbitration on "real or perceived problems of analytical tradecraft or politicization, biased reporting, or lack of objectivity" (§1020).

These efforts, however, are affected by the long lead times needed to prepare and train analysts, especially in such fields as counterterrorism and counterproliferation. Initiatives undertaken after the passage of the 2004 act should now have produced a mature cadre of analysts. At the same time, sensitivity to intelligence tradecraft and to the pitfalls of groupthink may have dulled in the years since the intelligence failure associated with Iraq's WMD program. The quality of intelligence community analysis may be tested by emerging national security challenges, such as those associated with Iran's nuclear program.

ISSUES IN THE 113TH CONGRESS

In addition to government-wide budgetary issues that have the potential for significant effects on intelligence activities, observers expect that oversight of the implementation of the Intelligence Reform Act will continue to be a concern for the 113th Congress. Congress continues to monitor the evolving relationship between the DNI and the CIA Director. The role and effectiveness of new or reformed post-9/11 intelligence elements—for example, the FBI, DHS Intelligence & Analysis, and the Under Secretary of Defense for

Intelligence—will likely continue to be areas of congressional interest. Future satellite procurement programs likely continue to be an important issue given the multi-billion dollar costs involved, though many of the details remain classified.

Unauthorized disclosures of classified information will likely continue to be a concern, despite recent executive branch efforts to address this problem. The committee comments in S.Rept. 112- 192 state their "grave concern" with "both the quantity and substance" of the disclosures, influencing the introduction of new provisions to prevent and detect future unauthorized disclosures. While no one agency or branch of government was believed to be more responsible than others, the committee called upon the executive branch to be vigilant and aggressively investigate and prosecute those found to be responsible.

The CIA's role in targeted killings may come under closer scrutiny, as the Administration and Members seek to balance a desire for increased transparency and accountability with the need to safeguard what many argue is an effective tool against al-Qaeda.

Benghazi

The attack in Benghazi on September 11, 2012, that claimed the lives of four Americans, including U.S. Ambassador to Libya John C. Stevens, raised a number of intelligence issues. As it pertained to Administration and intelligence community actions after the attack, public debate focused on two related but separate questions regarding whether the incident was a terrorist attack and whether there was a protest prior to the incident. The second question is more directly related to the analytic judgments of the intelligence community. According to public accounts provided by the news media, the intelligence community assessed incorrectly on September 12 that a protest had occurred. The community changed its assessment, based on new information, around September 20.[13] The DNI more than a week later publically acknowledged this change, stating, "As we learned more about the attack, we revised our initial assessment to reflect new information indicating that it was a deliberate and organized terrorist attack carried out by extremists."[14]

Defenders of the IC performance point out that analysts are often called on soon after an incident such as the one that occurred in Benghazi to make difficult judgments based on incomplete information. Those judgments can and should change as information becomes available that provides a more complete picture.[15] This is the nature of intelligence work. They also argue that the possible presence of a protest in Benghazi was just one of many challenging questions presented to analysts about the responsibility and implications of the attack.

As noted above, the performance of the intelligence community's analytical offices came into focus after the failure to provide advance warning of the 9/11 attacks and a flawed estimate of Iraqi weapons of mass destruction. Assessments of Benghazi offer an oversight opportunity for Congress to determine to what extent the intelligence community has improved its analytic tradecraft. Congressional oversight thus far has focused primarily on the Department of State's actions prior to the attack and on the Administration's public statements.

Britt Snider, in his book about intelligence oversight, argues that looking behind intelligence analysis has historically proven difficult for the intelligence committees. He notes, however, that "This is not to say the select committees cannot do independent evaluations of intelligence analysis or do them well. The HPSCI's 1979 report on the fall of the Shah in Iran and the SSCI's 2004 evaluation of the prewar assessments on Iraq are cases in point."[16] With respect to Benghazi, oversight questions that could be addressed include: Was the initial judgment that a protest had occurred valid given the information that was available as of September 12? Why was information about a protest considered credible at the time? Based on new information, should analysts have corrected their assessment earlier than September 20? Did analysts display "anchoring bias"—the tendency to give greater weight to early information and assessments?

Intelligence Agencies and Drone Warfare

U.S. counterterrorism efforts in Iraq, Afghanistan, Pakistan, and in other areas have been heavily dependent upon the use of unmanned aerial vehicles (UAVs) or unmanned aerial systems (UAS), referred to as "drones" in the media, for intelligence collection, often in real time. They provide important substitutes for, or supplements to, other intelligence platforms such as satellites and manned aircraft. In addition, some UAVs have been modified to launch weapons at designated targets. Operated remotely from ground stations in the region or even from the United States, armed UAVs can avoid the need to introduce U.S. personnel into direct combat, a significant advantage. Their use can also avoid the diplomatic complications of a ground-based U.S. military presence. UAVs are operated both by the military services and intelligence agencies depending on a number of operational and statutory considerations. Use by the military forces would be undertaken consistent with Title 10 authorities. 50 U.S.C. 413b provides statutory authorities for the DNI to undertake covert actions at presidential direction.

Many have expressed concern about reports of expanded use of UAVs in targeted attacks. Some observers suggest that some individuals may not be legitimate targets as envisioned by the 2001 Authorization for the Use of Force (P.L. 107-40), or believe that targeted attacks in countries where the United States is not otherwise engaged in armed conflict might violate international law. Since the September 2011 targeted killing of Anwar al-Awlaki, an American who fled to Yemen and became a senior leader within al-Qaeda in the Arabian Peninsula, many have questioned the legal basis of such a strike against a U.S. citizen. Still others question the effectiveness of the program over the long term and warn that drone attacks inside foreign countries such as Pakistan will encourage opposition to overall U.S. policy goals by engendering negative perceptions that ultimately bolster al-Qaeda's ranks. Former DNI Blair has stated: "in Pakistan, news media accounts of heavy civilian casualties are widely believed. Our reliance on high-tech strikes that pose no risk to our soldiers is bitterly resented in a country that cannot duplicate such feats of warfare without cost to its own troops." Congress is expected to maintain close oversight of the use of UAVs in the counterterrorism effort.

Role of the FBI

In the wake of the September 2001 attacks, the FBI was strongly criticized for failing to focus on the terrorist threat, for failing to collect and strategically analyze intelligence, and for failing to share intelligence with other intelligence agencies (as well as among various FBI components). Subsequently, FBI Director Robert S. Mueller III introduced a number of reforms to create a better and more professional intelligence effort in an agency that has always emphasized law enforcement. Congress has expressed concern about the overall effectiveness of these reforms and with the FBI's widely criticized information technology acquisition efforts.[17] These issues came into focus after the November 2009 Fort Hood shooting that claimed the lives of 13 Department of Defense employees. It was determined that the FBI had information about the shooter prior to the attack that it did not fully disseminate to DOD or the other members of the intelligence community. A Senate investigation into the shooting found that "the Fcrt Hood attack is an indicator that the current status of the FBI's transformation to become intelligence-driven is incomplete and that the FBI faces internal challenges - which may include cultural barriers - that can frustrate the on-going institutional reforms."[18]

Role of the DHS Office of Intelligence and Analysis

The Homeland Security Act of 2002 established within the Department of Homeland Security a Directorate for Information Analysis and Infrastructure Protection with the responsiblity to, among other things, "identify and assess the nature and scope of terrorist threats to the homeland" and "detect and identify threats of terrorism against the United States." The Directorate has since been broken into two components, with intelligence collection and analysis functions falling to the Office of Intelligence and Analysis (I&A). In addition, the Bush Administration announced the establishment of the Terrorist Threat Integration Center (TTIC) in January 2003 under the DCI. In accordance with Executive Order 13354 of August 27, 2004, and the Intelligence Reform Act, TTIC was transferred to the National Counterterrorism Center (NCTC), which constitutes the focal point for assessing information on potential terrorist threats from all sources.[19]

Some argue that the missions of these organizations are distinct. NCTC sits at the nexus between for foreign and domestic intelligence agencies, whereas I&A serves more as a liaison between federal, state and local partners and has a mandate beyond counterterrorism. Nonetheless, in light of the establishment of NCTC and the FBI's efforts to become an intelligence driven organization, Members have sometimes questioned the role and mission of DHS I&A.[20]

The Role of the Under Secretary of Defense for Intelligence

The position of Under Secretary of Defense for Intelligence (USD(I)) was established by the Defense Authorization Act for FY2003 (P.L. 107-314, §901). The statute and DOD directives give the incumbent significant authorities for the direction and control of intelligence agencies within DOD especially in regard to systems acquisition. There are reports that DOD special forces have also been involved in human intelligence collection efforts that are not effectively coordinated with CIA. Some media commentators have pointed to potential conflicts between the office of the USD(I) and the DNI's office. The first USD(I), Stephen Cambone, resigned at the end of 2006; his successor was retired Air Force Lieutenant General James Clapper, who previously served as director of both NGA and DIA and who became DNI in August 2010. Michael Vickers, who had previously served in the CIA, was nominated to serve as USD(I) in January 2011 and was confirmed by the Senate on March 17. In May 2007 the USD(I) was also designated Director of Defense Intelligence and also serves on the DNI's executive committee.

The USD(I) has considerable intelligence budgetary and hiring authority that sometimes rivals or exceeds that of the DNI. Some observers argue that the current working relationship between the DNI and the USD(I) is as much a result of personal relationships and temperament as it is a reflection of sound institutional arrangements between the two positions. Thus, the mission and responsibilities of the USD(I), and the institutional and statutory relationship with the DNI, may be areas of continued congressional interest.

Paramilitary Operations and Defense Humint

Some observers have expressed concern that expanded efforts by DOD intelligence personnel to collect humint overseas and undertake "preparation of the battlefield" operations may interfere with ongoing efforts of CIA humint collectors. Intelligence officials have maintained in congressional testimony that there is no unnecessary duplication of effort and that careful coordination is undertaken during the planning and implementing of such operations. The determination to ensure that such coordination is effective was further reflected in the designation of the DCIA as head of the National Clandestine Service. Members have also questioned the adequacy of DOD's administration of its intelligence personnel, citing cover problems, unproductive deployment locations, and "non-existent" career management.[21]

DOD in April 2012 announced the creation of a new Defense Clandestine Service intended to shift the defense intelligence activities away from tactical support and to focus more on humint operations against national-level priorities. A month later, the Senate Armed Services Committee, in its version of the National Defense Authorization Act of 2013, moved to constrain the growth of DOD's human intelligence personnel. The final bill froze funding for civilian personnel conducting defense human intelligence at the amount necessary to support the number of such personnel as of April 20, 2012.[22] The Senate report language accompanying its version of the bill stated:

> The committee notes that President Bush authorized 50 percent growth in the CIA's case officer workforce, which followed significant growth under President Clinton. Since 9/11, DOD's case officer ranks have grown substantially as well. The committee is concerned that, despite this expansion and the winding down of two overseas conflicts that required large HUMINT resources, DOD believes that its needs are not being met.[23]

Congressional Notification Procedures

The intelligence investigations of the 1970s led to eventual enactment of statutory provisions requiring that Congress be informed of covert actions as well as current and anticipated intelligence activities other than covert actions. These provisions require the Administration to keep the two intelligence committees "fully and currently informed" of intelligence activities and significant anticipated intelligence activities. Covert actions must be approved by the President and Congress must be notified, but special provisions were subsequently established to permit in extraordinary circumstances limiting notification of covert actions to the chairmen and ranking minority Members of the intelligence committees, the Speaker of the House and the House minority leader, and the majority and minority leaders of the Senate, the so-called "Gang of Eight." Whether Gang of Eight or even more limited notification can be used for intelligence activities other than covert actions has become a source of controversy in recent years with some Members arguing that the statutes require that all committee members be notified at least in the case of intelligence activities that are not covert actions. The House Intelligence Committee included a provision (§321) in its FY2010 intelligence authorization bill (H.R. 2701) that would remove the Gang of Eight provisions and require that all committee Members be briefed on all intelligence activities, including covert actions, unless the committee itself decided to limit notification. The Administration, in its Statement of Administration Policy issued July 8, 2009, stated firm opposition to Section 321, arguing that it "runs afoul of tradition by restricting an important established means by which the President protects the most sensitive intelligence activities."[24] The Senate version of the FY2010 intelligence authorization bill, which ultimately became

P.L. 111-259, addresses notification both of covert actions and intelligence activities generally; it requires that, if the Administration does not provide information to all Members of the two committees, it will be required to notify the committees of the reasons for withholding information and a description of the "main features" of the activity that can be made available to all committee members.

Members have continued to express frustration with the extent to which they are consulted or notified about intelligence activity, most recently during the Senate confirmation of John Brennan as CIA Director. That confirmation was held up while Members demanded to see Department of Justice Office of Legal Counsel opinions about the Administration's targeted killing program. Although such opinions are not governed by congressional notification procedures, some Members suggested that the initial refusal to share those opinions was indicative of distrust between the intelligence community and its oversight bodies.[25]

Information Security and Unauthorized Disclosures

Unauthorized disclosures of classified information, whether from a media source, government agency or employee, or anonymously, have received significant attention over the past year. The Senate Intelligence Authorization legislation, which passed the House in December and was signed by the President in January 2013, focused on tighter restrictions to prevent disclosures and define consequences. The anti-leak proposals limit interaction between the media and cleared personnel, require the intelligence community to develop an insider threat program, and allow the government to withhold the pension of those who illegally disclose classified data. The bill also revises the definition of "intelligence agency" to include all elements of the intelligence community.[26] Most of the provisions pertaining to unauthorized disclosure of classified information were dropped from the final bill.

The White House in December 2012 released its *National Strategy for Information Sharing and Safeguarding*, which called for structural and policy reforms to address unauthorized disclosures of classified information.[27] The DNI in June 2012 also announced new measures to combat those disclosures.[28] It remains to be seen whether these actions will be effective or whether stronger action will be needed.

Government Accountability Office and the Intelligence Community

The Government Accountability Office (GAO), a legislative branch agency, has statutory authorities to audit and investigate the receipt, disbursement, and application of public funds with a broad right of access to agency records and information. There are, however, specific exceptions that cover many intelligence activities by the CIA and other intelligence agencies. Although oversight of intelligence efforts is undertaken by the two congressional intelligence committees, some Members believe that the GAO should also have a role in intelligence efforts.[29] In recent years, intelligence authorization bills have included provisions expanding GAO's responsibilities in regard to intelligence agencies; both the Bush and Obama Administrations have resisted these proposals. Provisions for an expanded GAO role were included in both the Senate and House FY2011 Intelligence Authorization bill (S. 1494, §335; H.R. 2701, §335) despite Administration opposition.[30] On May 27, 2010, an amendment sponsored by Representative Eshoo was added to the FY2011 Defense Authorization bill (H.R. 5136, §923) on a floor vote that would have required the DNI to provide the GAO with all information necessary to conduct an analysis, evaluation, or investigation requested by one of the congressional intelligence committees. In addition, a separate section would have recognized that GAO audits of intelligence agencies could be requested by any congressional committee with appropriate jurisdiction. In such cases, information relating to intelligence sources and methods or covert actions may be redacted and provided only to the congressional intelligence committees. The version of H.R. 2701 that both the Senate and House approved in late September 2010 required that the DNI issue a written directive no later than May 2011 to govern access by GAO for information held by intelligence agencies. On April 29, 2011, the DNI issued Intelligence Community Directive Number 114, *Comptroller General Access to Intelligence Community Information* which contains provisions designed to encourage cooperation between GAO and intelligence agencies. The Directive states, however, that information will not be provided to support a GAO audit or review of core national intelligence capabilities and activities. The Directive went into effect on June 30, 2011.

GAO's response to ICD 114 stated that it was a "good start" to improving access to information in possession of the intelligence community but that some language in the directive, if interpreted broadly by intelligence agencies, "could significantly hinder GAO's ability to conduct related work that we are routinely requested by the Congress to do."[31] Congress may wish to examine how ICD 114 has been interpreted and to what extent it has improved GAO access.

APPENDIX A. ADDITIONAL BACKGROUND

The "INTs": Intelligence Disciplines

The intelligence community has been built around major agencies responsible for specific intelligence collection systems known as disciplines. Three major intelligence disciplines or "INTs"—signals intelligence (*sigint*), imagery intelligence (*imint*), and human intelligence (*humint*)—provide the most important information for analysts and absorb the bulk of the intelligence budget. Sigint collection is the responsibility of NSA at Fort Meade, MD. Sigint operations are classified, but there is little doubt that the need for intelligence on a growing variety of nations and groups that are increasingly using sophisticated and rapidly changing encryption systems requires a far different sigint effort than the one prevailing during the Cold War. Since the late 1990s a process of change in NSA's culture and methods of operations has been initiated, a change required by the need to target terrorist groups and affected by the proliferation of communications technologies and inexpensive encryption systems. Observers credit the then-Director of NSA, Lieutenant General Michael Hayden, who later became Director of the CIA in May 2006, with launching a long-overdue reorganization of the agency, and adapting it to changed conditions. Part of his initiative has involved early retirements for some NSA personnel and greater reliance on outsourcing many functions previously done by career personnel. Some of the initiatives relating to acquisition did not, however, meet their objectives.

A second major intelligence discipline, imagery or *imint*, is also facing profound changes. Imagery is collected in essentially three ways: by satellites, manned aircraft, and unmanned aerial vehicles (UAVs). The satellite program that covered the Soviet Union and acquired highly accurate intelligence concerning submarines, missiles, bombers, and other military targets is perhaps the greatest achievement of the U.S. intelligence community—it served as a foundation for defense planning and strategic planning that led to the end of the Cold War. In today's environment, there is a greater number of collection targets than existed during the Cold War and more satellites are required, especially those that can be maneuvered to collect information about a variety of targets. At the same time, the availability of high-quality commercial satellite imagery and its widespread use by federal agencies has raised questions about the extent to which coverage from the private sector can meet the requirements of intelligence agencies. High altitude UAVs such as the Global Hawk may also provide surveillance capabilities that overlap those of satellites.

The National Imagery and Mapping Agency (NIMA) was established in 1996 to manage imagery processing and dissemination previously undertaken by a number of separate agencies. NIMA was renamed the National Geospatial-Intelligence Agency (NGA) by the FY2004 Defense Authorization Act (P.L. 108-136). The goal of NGA is, according to the agency, to use imagery and other geospatial information "to describe, assess, and visually depict physical features and geographically referenced activities on the Earth."

Intelligence from human contacts—*humint*—is the oldest intelligence discipline and the one that is most often written about in the media. The CIA is the primary collector of humint, but the Defense Department also has responsibilities filled by defense attachés at embassies around the world and by other agents working on behalf of theater commanders. Many observers have argued that inadequate humint has been a systemic problem and contributed to the inability to gain prior knowledge of the 9/11 plots. In part, these criticisms reflect the changing nature of the international environment. During the Cold War, principal targets of U.S. humint collection were foreign government officials and military leaders. Intelligence agency officials working undercover as diplomats could approach potential contacts at receptions or in the context of routine embassy business. Today, however, the need is to seek information from clandestine terrorist groups or narcotics traffickers who do not appear at embassy social gatherings. Humint from such sources can be especially important as there may be little evidence of activities or intentions that can be gathered from imagery, and their communications may be carefully limited.

Placing U.S. intelligence officials in foreign countries under "nonofficial cover" (NOC) in businesses or other private capacities is possible, but it presents significant challenges to U.S. agencies. Administrative mechanisms are vastly more complicated than they are for officials formally attached to an embassy; special arrangements have to be made for pay, allowances, retirement, and healthcare. The responsibilities of operatives under nonofficial cover to the parent intelligence agency have to be reconciled with those to private employers, and there is an unavoidable potential for conflicts of interest or even corruption. Any involvement with terrorist groups or smugglers has a potential for major embarrassment to the U.S. government and, of course, physical danger to those immediately involved.

Responding to allegations that CIA agents may have been involved too closely with narcotics smugglers and human rights violators in Central America, the then-Director of Central Intelligence (DCI), John Deutch, established guidelines in 1995 (which remain classified) to govern the recruitment of informants with unsavory backgrounds. Although CIA officials maintain that no proposal for contacts with persons having potentially valuable information was disapproved, there was a widespread belief that the guidelines served to encourage a "risk averse" atmosphere at a time when information on terrorist plans, from whatever source, was urgently sought. The FY2002 Intelligence Authorization Act (P.L. 107-108) directed the DCI to rescind and replace the guidelines, and July 2002 press reports indicated that they had been replaced.

A major constraint on humint collection is the availability of personnel trained in appropriate languages. Cold War efforts required a supply of linguists in a relatively finite set of foreign languages, but the intelligence community now needs experts in a wider range of more obscure languages and dialects. Various approaches have been considered: use of civilian contract personnel, military reservists with language qualifications, and substantial bonuses for agency personnel who maintain their proficiency. The National Security Education Program, established in 1991, provides scholarships and career training for individuals in or planning to enter careers in agencies dealing with national security issues.

Other "INTs"

A fourth INT, measurement and signatures analysis—*masint*—has received greater emphasis in recent years. A highly technical discipline, masint involves the application of complicated analytical refinements to information collected by sigint and imint sensors. It also includes spectral imaging by which the identities and characteristics of objects can be identified on the basis of their reflection and absorption of light. Masint is undertaken by DIA and other DOD agencies. A key problem has been retaining personnel with expertise in masint systems who are offered more remunerative positions in private industry.

Another category of information, open source information—*osint* (newspapers, periodicals, pamphlets, books, radio, television, and Internet websites)—is increasingly important given requirements for information about many regions and topics (instead of the former concentration on political and military issues affecting a few countries). At the same time, requirements for translation, dissemination, and systematic analysis have increased, given the multitude of different areas and the volume of materials. Many observers believe that intelligence agencies should be more aggressive in using osint; some believe that the availability of osint may even reduce the need for certain collection efforts. The availability of osint also raises questions regarding the need for intelligence agencies to undertake collection, analysis, and dissemination of information that could be directly obtained by user agencies. Section 1052 of the Intelligence Reform Act expressed the sense of Congress that there should be an open source intelligence center to coordinate the collection, analysis, production, and dissemination of open source intelligence to other intelligence agencies. An Open Source Center was subsequently established, although it has been managed by CIA personnel.

Integrating the "INTs"

The "INTs" have been the pillars of the intelligence community's organizational structure, but analysis of threats requires that data from all the INTs be brought together and that analysts have ready access to all sources of data on a timely basis. This has proved in the past to be a substantial challenge because of technical problems associated with transmitting data and the need to maintain the security of information acquired from highly sensitive sources. Some argue that intelligence officials have tended to err on the side of maintaining the security of information even at the cost of not sharing essential data with those having a need to know. Section 1015 of the Intelligence Reform Act mandated the establishment of an Intelligence Sharing Environment (ISE) to facilitate the sharing of terrorism-related information.

A related problem has been barriers between foreign intelligence and law enforcement information. These barriers derived from the different uses of information collected by the two sets of agencies—foreign intelligence used for policymaking and military operations and law enforcement information to be used in judicial proceedings in the United States. A large part of the statutory basis for the "wall" between law enforcement and intelligence information was removed with passage of the USA PATRIOT Act of 2001 (P.L. 107-56), which made it possible to share law enforcement information with analysts in intelligence agencies, but long-established practices have not been completely overcome. The Homeland Security Act (P.L. 107-296) and the subsequent creation of the Terrorist Threat Integration Center (TTIC) established offices charged with combining information from both types of sources. Section 1021 of the Intelligence Reform Act made the new National Counterterrorism Center (NCTC), TTIC's successor, operating under the DNI specifically responsible for "analyzing and integrating all intelligence possessed or acquired by the United States Government pertaining to terrorism and counterterrorism [except purely domestic terrorism]."[32]

Intelligence Budget Process

For budgetary purposes, intelligence spending is divided between the National Intelligence Program (NIP; formerly the National Foreign Intelligence Program or NFIP) and the Military Intelligence Program (MIP). The MIP was established in September 2005 and includes all programs from the former Joint Military Intelligence Program, which encompassed DOD-wide intelligence programs and most programs from the former Tactical Intelligence and Related Activities (TIARA) category, which encompassed intelligence programs supporting the operating units of the armed services. The Program Executive for the MIP is the Under Secretary of Defense for Intelligence. The bulk of the $50+ billion in national intelligence spending has been "hidden" within the DOD budget. Spending for most intelligence programs is described in classified annexes to intelligence and national defense authorization and appropriations legislation. (Members of Congress have access to these annexes, but must make special arrangements to read them.)

Intelligence spending is authorized in intelligence authorization acts. When intelligence authorization legislation is not enacted (as was the case between FY2006 and FY2010), most intelligence spending is authorized by a "catch-all" provision in defense appropriations acts.[33]

For a number of years some Members sought to make public total amounts of intelligence and intelligence-related spending; floor amendments for that purpose were defeated in both chambers during the 105th Congress. In response, however, to a lawsuit filed under the Freedom of Information Act, DCI George Tenet stated on October 15, 1997, that the aggregate amount appropriated for intelligence and intelligence-related activities for FY1997 was $26.6 billion. He added that the Administration would continue "to protect from disclosure any and all subsidiary information concerning the intelligence budget." In March 1998, DCI Tenet announced that the FY1998 figure was $26.7 billion. Figures for FY1999 and subsequent years were not released. During consideration of intelligence reform legislation in 2004, the Senate at one point approved a version of a bill which would have required publication of the amount of the NIP; the House version did not include a similar provision and, with the Senate deferring to the House, the Intelligence Reform Act did not require making intelligence spending amounts public. Section 601 of P.L. 110-53, Implementing Recommendations of the 9/11 Commission Act of 2007, requires, however, that the DNI publicly disclose the aggregate amount of funds appropriated for the NIP although after FY2008 the President could waive or postpone the disclosure upon sending an explanation to congressional oversight committees. Consistent with that act, the DNI announced in October 2008 that the aggregate amount appropriated to the National Intelligence Program for FY2008 was $47.5 billion. A year later the NIP for FY2009 was announced as $49.8 billion. In September 2009, DNI Blair stated publicly that total annual intelligence spending is $75 billion, a figure that includes not only the NIP but also military intelligence activities. In October 2010, the DNI announced that the amount appropriated to the NIP for FY2010 was $53.1 billion. Subsequently, DOD announced that the MIP appropriations for FY2010 was $27 billion, including both the base budget and supplemental appropriations. The amount appropriated for MIP in FY2011 was $24 billion, a $3 billion reduction from the year earlier. The amount appropriated for the NIP in FY2011 was $54.6 billion according to an October 2011 announcement. The amount appropriated to the NIP for FY2012 was $53.9 billion, according to an October 2012 announcement from the DNI. The amount requested for the NIP for FY2013 was $52.6 billion. According to a December 2012 statement from the leaders of the congressional intelligence committees, the FY2013 intelligence authorization bill is below 2012's enacted budget but slightly above the President's 2013 request.

Jurisdiction over intelligence programs is somewhat different in the House and the Senate. The Senate Intelligence Committee has jurisdiction only over the NIP but not the MIP, whereas the House Intelligence Committee has jurisdiction over both sets of programs. The preponderance of intelligence spending is accomplished by intelligence agencies within DOD and thus in both chambers the armed services committees are involved in the oversight process. Other oversight committees are responsible for intelligence agencies that are part of departments over which they have jurisdiction.

Most appropriations for intelligence activities are included in national defense appropriations acts, including funds for the CIA, DIA, NSA, the NRO, and NGA. Other appropriations measures include funds for the intelligence offices of the State Department, the FBI, and DHS and other intelligence agencies. Although funds for CIA have been included in defense appropriations acts, these monies are transferred directly to the CIA Director. The Senate voted in October 2004 to establish an Appropriations Subcommittee on Intelligence, but this has not occurred nor did the House take similar action. On January 9, 2007, however, the House approved H.Res. 35, which established a select panel within the appropriations committee that includes three members of the intelligence committee to oversee appropriations for intelligence program. The select panel was not continued in the 112th Congress.

Intelligence budgeting issues were at the center of the debate on intelligence reform legislation in 2004. On one hand, there was determination to make the new DNI responsible for developing and determining the annual National Intelligence Program budget (which is separate from the MIP budgets that are prepared by the Office of the Secretary of Defense). The goal was to ensure a unity of effort that arguably has not previously existed and that may have complicated efforts to monitor terrorist activities. On the other hand, the intelligence efforts within the National Intelligence Program include those of major components of the Defense Department, including NSA, the NRO, and NGA, that are closely related to other military activities. Some Members thus argued that even the National Intelligence Program should not be considered apart from the Defense budget. After considerable debate, the final version of P.L. 108-458 provides broad budgetary authorities to the DNI, but in Section 1018 requires the President to issue guidelines to ensure that the DNI exercises the authorities provided by the statute "in a manner that respects and does not abrogate the statutory responsibilities of the heads of" the Office of Management and Budget and Cabinet departments. Observers expect that implementing the complex and seemingly overlapping budgetary provisions of the Intelligence Reform Act will continue to depend on effective working relationships among the Office of the DNI, DOD, and the White House staff. In late 2011 Congress passed the FY2012 Intelligence Authorization bill (H.R. 1892) and the Consolidated Appropriations Act, 2012 (P.L. 112-74). The two acts contained provisions affecting intelligence budgeting. Section 433 of the former authorizes the establishment of Treasury Department accounts to receive funds from defense intelligence elements, the ODNI, and other agencies for authorized programs. The latter contains several provisions (especially Sections 8090, 8092, and 8094) that would bring intelligence budget submissions into alignment with formats established for the Defense Department. Taken together, the provisions may facilitate the DNI's management of intelligence accounts and strengthen congressional oversight even though an earlier initiative by DNI Clapper for the submission of a NIP budget request separate from the DOD budget is precluded (§8116).

The 9/11 Investigations and the Congressional Response

In the aftermath of September 11, 2001, there was extensive public discussion of whether the attacks on the Pentagon and World Trade Center represented an "intelligence failure." In response, the Senate Select Committee on Intelligence and the House Permanent Select Committee on Intelligence undertook a joint investigation of the September 11 attacks. Public hearings by the resulting "Joint Inquiry" were launched on September 18, 2002, beginning with testimony from representatives of families of those who died in the attacks. Former policymakers and senior CIA and FBI officials also testified. Eleanor Hill, the inquiry staff director, summarized the inquiry's findings:

> the Intelligence Community did have general indications of a possible terrorist attack against the United States or U.S. interests overseas in the spring and summer of 2001 and promulgated strategic warnings. However, it does not appear that the Intelligence Community had information prior to September 11 that identified precisely where, when and how the attacks were to be carried out.

The two intelligence committees published the findings and conclusions of the Joint Inquiry on December 11, 2002.[34] The committees found that the intelligence community had received, beginning in 1998 and continuing into the summer of 2001, "a modest, but relatively steady, stream of intelligence reporting that indicated the possibility of terrorist attacks within the United States." Further findings dealt with specific terrorists about whom some information had come to the attention of U.S. officials prior to September 11 and with reports about possible employment of civilian airliners to crash into major buildings. The inquiry also made systemic findings highlighting the intelligence community's lack of preparedness to deal with the challenges of global terrorism, inefficiencies in budgetary planning, the lack of adequate numbers of linguists, a lack of human sources, and an unwillingness to share information among agencies.

Separately, the two intelligence committees submitted recommendations for strengthening intelligence capabilities. They urged the creation of a Cabinet-level position of Director of National Intelligence (DNI) separate from the position of director of the CIA. The DNI would have greater budgetary and managerial authority over intelligence agencies in the Defense Department than possessed by the DCI. The committees also expressed great concern with the reorientation of the FBI to counterterrorism and suggested consideration of the creation of a new domestic surveillance agency similar to Britain's MI5.

The Joint Inquiry was focused directly on the performance of intelligence agencies, but there was widespread support among Members for a more extensive review of the roles of other government agencies. Provisions for establishing an independent commission on the 2001 terrorist attacks were included in the FY2003 Intelligence Authorization Act (P.L. 107-306). Former New Jersey Governor Thomas H. Kean was named to serve as chairman, with former Representative Lee H. Hamilton serving as vice chairman. Widely publicized hearings were held in spring 2004 with Administration and outside witnesses providing different perspectives on the role of intelligence agencies prior to the September 11, 2001, attacks. The commission's report was published in July 2004.

Although the 9/11 Commission surveyed the roles of a number of federal and local agencies, many of its principal recommendations concerned the perceived lack of authorities of the DCI. The commission recommended establishing a National Intelligence Director (NID) to manage the National Intelligence Program and oversee the agencies that contribute to it. The NID would annually submit a national intelligence program budget and, when necessary, forward the names of nominees to be heads of major intelligence agencies to the President. Lead responsibility for conducting and executing paramilitary operations would be assigned to DOD and not CIA. The commission also recommended that Congress pass a separate annual appropriations act for intelligence that would be made public. The NID would execute the expenditure of appropriated funds and make transfers of funds or personnel as appropriate. Proposing a significant change in congressional practice, the commission recommended a single intelligence committee in each house of Congress, combining authorizing and appropriating authorities.

On August 27, 2004, President Bush addressed key recommendations of the 9/11 Commission in signing several executive orders to reform intelligence. In addition to establishing a National Counterterrorism Center, the orders provided new authorities for the DCI until legislation was enacted to create a National Intelligence Director. In addition, several legislative proposals were introduced to establish a National Intelligence Director, separate from a CIA Director. The Senate passed S. 2845 on October 16, 2004;

the House had passed H.R. 10 on October 8, 2004. Efforts by the resulting conference committee to reach agreed-upon text focused on the issue of the authorities of the proposed Director of National Intelligence in regard to the budgets and operations of the major intelligence agencies in DOD, especially NSA, NRO, and NGA. Conferees finally reached agreement in early December, and the conference report on S. 2845 (H.Rept. 108-796) was approved by the House on December 7 and by the Senate on December 8. The President signed the legislation on December 17, 2004, and it became P.L. 108-458.

The Intelligence Reform Act is wide-ranging, and its ongoing implementation will continue to receive oversight during the 113th Congress. Some observers have suggested that modifications to the legislation may be needed; others recommend that any difficulties be addressed by executive orders or memoranda of understanding.

Terrorist Surveillance Program/NSA Electronic Surveillance/FISA

In December 2005 media accounts of electronic surveillance by NSA authorized outside the parameters of the Foreign Intelligence Surveillance Act (FISA) led to extensive criticism of the Administration. Although the technical details of the effort remain classified, the Bush Administration maintained that communications, which involve a party reasonably considered to be a member of Al Qaeda, or affiliated with Al Qaeda, and one party in the United States, may be monitored on the basis of the President's constitutional authorities and the provisions of the Joint Resolution providing for Authority for the Use of Force (P.L. 107-40) of September 18, 2001. The need for speed and agility required, the Administration further argued, an approach not envisioned by the drafters of FISA. Others countered that FISA should have governed such electronic surveillance. In early March 2006 agreement was reached with the leadership of the two intelligence committees to establish procedures for enhanced legislative oversight of the NSA effort, and legislative initiatives were considered to either modify FISA or establish new statutory authorities for electronic surveillance.

Differing views of Members on the NSA effort were reflected in the House Intelligence Committee's 2006 report on FY2007 intelligence authorization legislation (H.Rept. 109-411). In light of decisions issued by the Foreign Intelligence Surveillance Court (FISC) on January 10, 2007, the Bush

Administration advised the chairman and ranking Member of the Senate Judiciary Committee that any electronic surveillance that had previously occurred as part of the Terrorist Surveillance Program (TSP) would thereafter be conducted subject to the approval of the FISC. Further, the Administration indicated that it would not re-authorize the TSP after the expiration of the then-current authorization. On May 1, 2007, the Senate Intelligence Committee held an open hearing on the Administration's proposal to revise FISA to take account of changes in communications technologies since the 1970s, with Members expressing differing views on the desirability of the legislation.

According to media reports, a judge on the FISC at some point in 2007 ruled that a FISC order was required for surveillance of communications between foreign persons abroad if the communications passed through the United States. On August 2, 2007, the DNI issued a statement on FISA modernization in which he contended that the intelligence community "should not be required to obtain court orders to effectively collect foreign intelligence from foreign targets located overseas." Although details of the effort remain classified, there appears to have been wide agreement among Members that FISA needed to be amended to permit surveillance without a court order of such foreign to foreign communications regardless of whether they were routed through the United States.

The Protect America Act (PAA) (P.L. 110-55), signed on August 5, 2007, after extensive congressional debate, excluded from the definition of "electronic surveillance" under FISA surveillance directed at a person reasonably believed to be located outside the United States. In addition, under certain circumstances, FISA, as amended by this legislation, permitted the DNI and the Attorney General, for periods up to one year, to authorize acquisition of foreign intelligence information "concerning persons reasonably believed to be located outside of the United States," apparently including U.S. persons, and to direct a communications provider, custodian, or other person with access to the communication immediately to provide information, facilities, and assistance to accomplish the acquisition. Those receiving such directives had the right to contest them in court. The DNI and the Attorney General were required to certify, in part, that this acquisition did not constitute electronic surveillance, and the Attorney General was required to submit the procedures by which this determination is made to the FISC for review as to whether the government determination was clearly erroneous. On a semiannual basis, the Attorney General was to report to congressional oversight committees on instances of noncompliance with directives and numbers of certifications and directives issued during the reporting period. P.L. 110-55 expired on February 1, 2008, and efforts to extend it further failed in the House when H.R. 5349 was rejected on February 13. Acquisitions authorized while the PAA was in force may continue until the expiration of the period for which they were authorized.

The Protect America Act was strongly criticized by some Members; on November 15, 2007, H.R. 3773, the RESTORE Act (the Responsible Electronic Surveillance that is Overseen, Reviewed, and Effective Act of 2007) was passed by the House in an attempt to clarify that a court order is not required for the acquisition of the contents of communications between two persons neither of whom is known to be a U.S. person, and both of whom are reasonably believed to be located outside the United States, regardless of whether the communications passed through the United States or if the surveillance device was in the United States. If, in the course of such an acquisition, the communications of a U.S. person were incidentally intercepted, stringent minimization procedures would have applied. Court orders would, however, have been required if the communications of a non-U.S. person reasonably believed to be located outside the United States were targeted where the other parties to the target's communications are unknown and thus might include U.S. persons or persons located physically in the United States. Some Members argued that this provision would unnecessarily tie the hands of intelligence agencies and jeopardize the counterterrorism effort. The RESTORE Act would have also provided for increased judicial oversight and would have required quarterly implementation and compliance audits by the Inspector General of the Justice Department, and added related congressional reporting requirements.

On October 26, 2007, the Senate Intelligence Committee reported its own version of a FISA amendment. The Senate bill (S. 2248), as amended, contained provisions authorizing the Attorney General and the DNI jointly to authorize targeting of persons, other than U.S. persons, reasonably believed to be outside the United States to acquire foreign intelligence information for periods up to one year. Under the Senate bill, FISC approval would have been required for targeting a U.S. person reasonably believed to be located outside the United States to acquire foreign intelligence information, if the acquisition constitutes electronic surveillance under FISA, or the acquisition of stored electronic communications or stored electronic data that requires an order under FISA, and the acquisition is conducted in the United States. The Senate bill would have also provided some retroactive immunity to telecommunications companies from civil suits in federal and states courts related to assistance that they have provided to the government in connection with intelligence activities between September 11, 2001, and January 17, 2007.

A central issue was the role of the judicial branch, and the Foreign Intelligence Surveillance Court (FISC) in particular, in approving and/or overseeing surveillance that does not target but may involve individuals who are U.S. persons. Some argued that only the independent judiciary could ensure that intelligence efforts would not become improperly or illegally directed towards Americans. At the time FISA permitted electronic surveillance to gather foreign intelligence information pursuant to a FISC order of U.S. persons where there was probable cause to believe they were foreign powers or agents of foreign powers if other statutory criteria were met. Some argued, however, that changes in technologies since FISA was enacted in 1978 made case-by-case judicial review of each international communication link that might involve a U.S. person impractical and risky to national security. Details of this issue are complex and, in many cases, classified. The Senate approved S. 2248 on February 12, 2008 (and incorporated it into H.R. 3773).

On March 14, 2008, the House approved an amendment to the version of H.R. 3773 that had been approved by the Senate. The House amendment would have required judicial review by the FISC of procedures for targeting a non-U.S. person located outside of the United States even if the person was not reasonably believed to be communicating with a U.S. person or a person in the United States. The House amendment would have required either a prior FISC order approving the applicable certification, targeting procedures, and minimization procedures or a determination that an emergency situation exists in which case a certification would have to be filed with the FISC within seven days. The Bush Administration argued that this requirement added unprecedented requirements for targeting communications of non-U.S. persons that could result in delaying collection efforts and the loss of some intelligence forever.

If the target of an acquisition were a U.S. person reasonably believed to be outside the United States, then, except in emergencies, the House-passed amendment would have required a FISC order approving an application for an acquisition for a period up to 90 days. The acquisition could have been renewed for additional 90-day periods upon submission of renewal applications. If the Attorney General authorized an emergency acquisition of such a U.S. person's communications, the Attorney General would have had to submit an application for a court order within seven days of that authorization.

The House version of H.R. 3773 would also not have granted retroactive immunity to telecommunications companies but would have allowed them to present evidence in their defense to a court. In addition, the House bill would have established a commission on warrantless electronic surveillance activities conducted between September 11, 2001, and January 17, 2007. The House version of H.R. 3773 did not come to a vote in the Senate and, after considerable discussions, Representative Reyes introduced a new bill, H.R. 6304, on June 19, 2008, that strengthened the role of the FISC in approving procedures for intelligence surveillance and provided telecommunications companies an opportunity to demonstrate to the courts that they had acted in response to a request for support from the executive branch. H.R. 6304 was passed by the House on June 20, 2008, and by the Senate on July 9, 2008; it was signed by the President on July 10, becoming P.L. 110-261.

At the end of 2009 three FISA provisions, dealing with "Lone Wolf" terrorists, roving wiretaps, and access to business records, were set to expire unless extended. They were extended until February 28, 2010, by a provision of the Defense Appropriations Act for FY2010 (P.L. 111-118) and separate legislation (P.L. 111-141) extended them until February 28, 2011. They were subsequently extended until May 27, 2011, by P.L. 112-3, and until June 1, 2015, by P.L. 112-14.

APPENDIX B. FOR ADDITIONAL READING

U.S. Commission on the Intelligence Capabilities of the United States Regarding Weapons of Mass Destruction, *Report to the President of the United States*, March 31, 2005.

U.S. Congress. Committee of Conference Intelligence Authorization Act for Fiscal Year 2005: Conference Report. December 7, 2004. 108th Congress, 2nd session (H.Rept. 108-798).

——. *Intelligence Reform and Terrorism Prevention Act of 2004.* December 7, 2004. 108th Congress, 2nd session. (H.Rept. 108-796).

U.S. Congress. House of Representatives. Permanent Select Committee on Intelligence. Report of the U.S. Senate Select Committee on Intelligence and U.S. House Permanent Select Committee on Intelligence, *Joint Inquiry into Intelligence Community Activities Before and After the Terrorist Attacks of September 11, 2001.* December 2002. 107th Congress, 2nd session (H.Rept. 107-792). [Also, S.Rept. 107-351]

——. *Intelligence Authorization Act for Fiscal Year 2005*. June 21, 2004. 108th Congress, 2nd session (H.Rept. 108-558).

——. *Intelligence Authorization Act for Fiscal Year 2006*. June 2, 2005. 109th Congress, 1st session (H.Rept. 109-101).

——. *Intelligence Authorization Act for Fiscal Year 2007*. April 6, 2006. 109th Congress, 2nd session (H.Rept. 109-411).

——. *Intelligence Authorization Act for Fiscal Year 2008*. May 7, 2007. 110th Congress, 1st session (H.Rept. 110-131).

——. *Intelligence Authorization Act for Fiscal Year 2008*. Conference Report. December 6, 2007. 110th Congress, 1st session (H.Rept. 110-478).

——. *Intelligence Authorization Act for Fiscal Year 2009*. May 21, 2008. 110th Congress, 2nd session (H.Rept. 110-665).

——. *Intelligence Authorization Act for Fiscal Year 2010*. June 26, 2009. 111th Congress, 1st session (H.Rept. 111-186).

——. *Intelligence Authorization Act for Fiscal Year 2011*. May 3, 2011. 112th Congress 1st session (H.Rept. 112-72).

——. *Intelligence Authorization Act for Fiscal Year 2012*. September 2, 2011. 112th Congress 1st session (H.Rept. 112-197). (Text of Managers Amendment printed in *Congressional Record*, December 14, 2011, pp. S8613-8617.)

——. Subcommittee on Terrorism and Homeland Security. *Counterterrorism Intelligence Capabilities and Performance Prior to 9-11*. July 2002.

U.S. Congress. Senate. Select Committee on Intelligence. *Report of the Select Committee on Intelligence on the U.S. Intelligence Community's Prewar Intelligence Assessments on Iraq*. July 9, 2004. 108th Congress, 2nd session (S.Rept. 108-301).

——. *Intelligence Authorization Act for Fiscal Year 2006*. September 29, 2005. 109th Congress, 1st session (S.Rept. 109-142).

——. *To authorize Appropriations for Fiscal Year 2005 for Intelligence and Intelligence-Related Activities of the United States Government, the Intelligence Community Management Account, and the Central Intelligence Agency Retirement and Disability System*. May 5, 2004. 108th Congress, 2nd session (S.Rept. 108-258).

——. *Intelligence Authorization Act for Fiscal Year 2007*. January 24, 2007. 110th Congress, 1st session (S.Rept. 110-2).

——. *Intelligence Authorization Act for Fiscal Year 2008*. May 31, 2007. 110th Congress, 1st session (S.Rept. 110-75).

——. *Intelligence Authorization Act for Fiscal Year 2009*. May 8, 2008, 110th Congress, 2nd session (S.Rept. 110-333).

——. *Intelligence Authorization Act for Fiscal Year 2010*. July 22, 2009 [S.1494]. 111th Congress, 1st session (S.Rept. 111-55).

——. *Intelligence Authorization Act for Fiscal Year 2010*. July 19, 2010 [S.3611]. 111th Congress, 2nd session (S.Rept. 111-223).

——. *Intelligence Authorization Act for Fiscal Year 2011*. April 4, 2011 [S.719]. 112th Congress, 1st session (S.Rept. 112-12).

——. *Intelligence Authorization Act for Fiscal Year 2012*. August 1, 2011 [S.1458]. 112th Congress, 1st session (S.Rept. 112-43).

——. *Intelligence Authorization Act for Fiscal Year 2013*. July 30, 2012 [S.3454]. 112th Congress, 2nd session (S.Rept. 112-192).

——. *Report of the Select Committee on Intelligence United States Senate covering the period from January 5, 2011 to January 3, 2013*. March 22, 2013. 1123th Congress, 1st session (S.Rept. 113-7).

——. *Unclassified Executive Summary of the Committee Report on the Attempted Terrorist Attack on Northwest Airlines Flight 253*. May 18, 2010.

U.S. Department of Justice, Commission for Review of FBI Security Programs, *A Review of FBI Security Programs*, March 2002.

U.S. National Commission on Terrorist Attacks Upon the United States. *The 9/11 Commission Report*, July 2004.

End Notes

[1] See Senate Select Committee on Intelligence hearing on "Security Threats to the United States," March 12, 2013.

[2] White House Review Summery Regarding 12/25/2009 Attempted Terrorist Attack, January 7, 2010.

[3] Questions & Answers on the Intelligence Community Post 9/11, Office of the Director of National Intelligence, July 19, 2010.

[4] White House Review Summery Regarding 12/25/2009 Attempted Terrorist Attack, January 7, 2010.

[5] Senate Select Committee on Intelligence, Additional Prehearing Questions for. Mr. John O. Brennan upon his nominiation to be the Director of the Central Intelligence Agency.

[6] See for example, the Webster Commission and Senate Homeland Security and Government Affairs Committee reports on the 2009 Fort Hood shooting.

[7] "Unclassified Executive Summary of teh Committee Report on the Attempted Terrorist Attack on Northwest Airlines Flight 253," Senate Select Committee on Intelligence, May 18, 2010.

[8] FINAL REPORT of the WILLIAM H. WEBSTER COMMISSION on The Federal Bureau of Investigation, Counterterrorism Intelligence, and the Events at Fort Hood, Texas, on November 5, 2009.

[9] For example, the National Counterterrorism Center established "pursuit teams"—groups of analyst who are not responsible for producing finished intelligence for policymakers and whose responsibility is it follow-up terrorism leads.

[10] Greg Miller, "Secret Report Raises Alarms on Intelligence Blind Spots because of AQ focus," The Washington Post, March 20, 2013.

[11] Senate Select Intelligence Committee, Confirmation Hearing on the Nomination of John O. Brennan to be CIA Director, February 7, 2013

[12] Paul Pillar, "Intelligence and Public Perceptions of It," The National Interest, March 27, 2013, available at http://nationalinterest.org/blog/paul-pillar/intelligence-public-perceptions-it-8283.

[13] Adam Entous and Siobhan Gorman, "Intelligence Stressed Libya Protest Scenario," The Wall Street Journal, October 22, 2012.

[14] Statement by the Director of Public Affairs for ODNI, Shawn Turner, on the intelligence related to the terrorist attack on the U.S. Consulate in Benghazi, Libya, September 28, 2012.

[15] See for example Aki Pertiz, "How Critics of Obama's Libya Response Profoundly Misunderstand Intelligence," The Atlantic, October 2, 2012.

[16] Britt Snyder, The Agency and the Hill: The CIA's Relationship with Congress, 1946 – 2004, The Center for the Study of Intelligence, p. 221.

[17] For further information, see CRS Report R41780, The Federal Bureau of Investigation and Terrorism Investigations, by Jerome P. Bjelopera.

[18] "A Ticking Time Bomb: Counterterrorism Lessons from the U.S. Government's Failure to Prevent the Fort Hood Attack," The Senate Homeland Security and Government Affairs Committee, February 2011.

[19] See CRS Report R41022, The National Counterterrorism Center (NCTC)—Responsibilities and Potential Congressional Concerns, by Richard A. Best Jr.

[20] See for example House Homeland Security Subcommittee on Intelligence, Information Sharing and Terrorism Risk Assessment hearing on "Homeland Security Department Intelligence Efforts", May 12, 2010.

[21] S.Rept. 112-173.

[22] P.L. 112-81.

[23] S.Rept. 112-173.

[24] CRS Report R40691, Sensitive Covert Action Notifications: Oversight Options for Congress. See also CRS Report R40698, "Gang of Four" Congressional Intelligence Notifications.

[25] See for example comments from Senator Rockefeller during the Senate Select Committee on Intelligence hearing on "Security Threats to the United States," March 12, 2013.

[26] U.S. Congress, 112th Congress, 2nd session, Senate, Select Committee on Intelligence, Intelligence Authorization Act for Fiscal Year 2013, S.Rept. 112-192, July 30, 2012, p. 13, Section 606, refers to Section 3(4) of the National Security Act.

[27] NATIONAL STRATEGY FOR INFORMATION SHARING AND SAFEGUARDING, December 2012.

[28] Director Clapper Announces Steps to Deter and Detect Unauthorized Disclosures, June 25, 2012.

[29] See CRS Report RL32525, Congressional Oversight of Intelligence: Current Structure and Alternatives, by L. Elaine Halchin and Frederick M. Kaiser, and "GAO Versus the CIA: Uphill Battles Against an Overpowering Force," International Journal of Intelligence and

Counterintelligence, Fall 2002. Similar proposals have been introduced over a long period, including stand-alone legislation such as S. 385, introduced by Senator Daniel Akaka in the 111th Congress, S. 82, in the 110th congress also introduced by Senator Akaka, and H.R. 978 introduced by Representative Bennie Thompson, and H.R. 3603 in the 100th Congress, introduced by then-Representative Leon Panetta.

[30] Office of Management and Budget, Statement of Administration Policy, H.R. 2701, Intelligence Authorization Act for Fiscal Year 2010, July 8, 2009.

[31] GAO Comments on Intelligence Community Directive Number 114, United States Government Accountability Office, April 29, 2011.

[32] See CRS Report R41022, The National Counterterrorism Center (NCTC)—Responsibilities and Potential Congressional Concerns, by Richard A. Best Jr.

[33] See CRS Report R40240, Intelligence Authorization Legislation: Status and Challenges, by Marshall Curtis Erwin. The FY2010 Intelligence Authorization Act (P.L. 111-259) was not enacted prior to the end of FY2010 and did not authorize FY2010 intelligence programs although it had significant legislative provisions.

[34] The full report was released some months later as H.Rept. 107-792/S.Rept. 107-351.

INDEX

#

21st century, x, 63
9/11, viii, x, 2, 3, 4, 16, 18, 19, 20, 21, 22, 25, 26, 56, 64, 65, 70, 73, 75, 79, 83, 87, 89, 90, 97
9/11 Commission, viii, 2, 4, 16, 18, 19, 20, 21, 22, 25, 26, 56, 65, 87, 90, 97

A

access, 4, 34, 37, 41, 47, 51, 53, 70, 81, 85, 86, 92, 95
accountability, 17, 74
acquisitions, 48, 49, 53, 55, 58
adaptability, 56
adjustment, 4, 5, 7, 38
advisory body, 37
Afghanistan, 12, 24, 30, 31, 32, 40, 43, 44, 47, 50, 51, 57, 59, 71, 75
agencies, viii, x, xi, 2, 10, 12, 13, 14, 15, 19, 29, 32, 35, 37, 38, 45, 48, 53, 57, 63, 64, 66, 67, 68, 69, 70, 72, 76, 77, 81, 82, 83, 84, 85, 87, 88, 89, 90, 91, 93
agility, 91
Air Force, 13, 37, 38, 39, 41, 42, 43, 44, 45, 51, 58, 59, 60, 66, 78
Al Qaeda, 91
anchoring, 75
appetite, 19
appropriations, vii, viii, 1, 2, 4, 13, 14, 15, 16, 17, 18, 19, 20, 21, 22, 23, 25, 36, 38, 41, 51, 52, 53, 54, 56, 57, 68, 86, 87, 90
Appropriations Act, 16, 18, 25, 60, 61, 95
Appropriations Committee, 19, 20, 21, 22, 23, 24, 53
Arabian Peninsula, 76
arbitration, 73
armed conflict, 76
armed forces, 72
arms control, 29, 31
assessment, 9, 41, 45, 74, 75
assets, 43, 51, 55
atmosphere, 84
Attorney General, 92, 93, 94
audit(s), 69, 81, 93
authority(s), viii, ix, x, 2, 10, 11, 12, 14, 15, 19, 20, 24, 25, 28, 37, 45, 63, 65, 67, 69, 70, 76, 77, 78, 81, 88, 90, 91
authorized programs, 88

B

barriers, 70, 77, 85
base, 4, 5, 34, 35, 41, 50, 87
benchmarks, 53
bias, 75
bonuses, 84
Bosnia, 31
Britain, 90
budget allocation, 12, 17

budget cuts, viii, x, 2, 9, 28, 55
bureaucracy, 31
Bush, President, 79, 90
business model, 39
businesses, 83

C

Cabinet, viii, 2, 30, 45, 66, 88, 89
cables, 41
certification, 94
challenges, viii, ix, x, 9, 15, 27, 28, 32, 43, 46, 49, 52, 55, 63, 64, 72, 73, 77, 83, 89
Chief of Staff, 58
CIA, x, 10, 12, 13, 14, 16, 24, 25, 30, 63, 66, 67, 68, 70, 71, 72, 73, 74, 78, 79, 80, 81, 82, 83, 84, 85, 87, 89, 90, 98
cities, 32
classification, 16, 22
Coast Guard, 13, 66, 68
Cold War, vii, 1, 9, 30, 33, 34, 43, 72, 82, 83, 84
collaboration, x, 64
commerce, 47
commercial, 34, 35, 36, 38, 39, 44, 45, 47, 49, 59, 72, 83
communication, 38, 92
community(s), viii, ix, x, 2, 3, 9, 10, 11, 12, 13, 15, 19, 20, 24, 28, 29, 38, 45, 46, 47, 49, 50, 55, 57, 63, 65, 66, 67, 69, 70, 71, 72, 73, 74, 77, 80, 81, 82, 84, 85, 89, 92
competition, 49, 70
complement, 38
complexity, 9, 29, 35, 39, 54
compliance, 93
complications, ix, 27, 56, 76
composition, 33
conference, 18, 38, 54, 91
Conference Report, 95, 96
conflict, 40
congress, 25, 61, 99
congressional budget, 16
consensus, ix, 28, 72
consent, 22
Consolidated Appropriations Act, 14, 18, 88
consumers, x, 29, 63
contingency, 9, 51
controversial, 18
conversations, 22
cooperation, x, 57, 63, 81
coordination, x, 31, 49, 53, 56, 63, 65, 78
corruption, 84
cost, ix, 9, 27, 29, 30, 31, 35, 36, 42, 44, 48, 49, 52, 54, 56, 76, 85
cost constraints, 56
cost controls, 36
counsel, 73
counterterrorism, ix, x, xi, 3, 12, 24, 27, 29, 32, 64, 67, 68, 69, 71, 72, 73, 75, 76, 77, 86, 90, 93
covering, 97
creep, 49
crises, 9
criticism, 69, 91
CT, 32
culture, 82
customers, 34, 35
cyber-attack, 9
cycles, 56

D

data processing, 56
DCI, 6, 10, 11, 23, 24, 77, 84, 86, 90
DEA, 13
decision makers, viii, 2, 3, 9, 47
deficiencies, 53
Department of Defense, viii, 2, 18, 19, 20, 22, 23, 25, 29, 43, 55, 57, 58, 59, 60, 61, 67, 68, 76
Department of Energy, 66
Department of Homeland Security, 24, 66, 68, 77
Department of Justice, 80, 97
Department of the Treasury, 66
depth, 68, 72
DHS, 13, 68, 73, 77, 87
directives, 77, 92

Director of National Intelligence, viii, ix, x, 2, 3, 4, 22, 23, 24, 25, 28, 51, 55, 58, 63, 64, 65, 66, 69, 89, 91, 97
disappointment, 52, 54
disbursement, 81
disclosure, vii, xi, 1, 3, 23, 64, 80, 86
divergence, 9
diversity, 8
DNI, viii, x, 2, 3, 4, 5, 9, 10, 11, 12, 14, 15, 16, 17, 18, 19, 21, 22, 23, 25, 28, 36, 37, 45, 48, 51, 52, 53, 55, 58, 63, 64, 65, 67, 69, 70, 71, 73, 74, 76, 78, 80, 81, 86, 87, 88, 89, 92, 93
DOD, viii, 2, 4, 5, 6, 8, 9, 11, 15, 16, 18, 19, 22, 23, 25, 29, 32, 33, 34, 37, 38, 39, 40, 41, 42, 45, 46, 47, 48, 49, 50, 51, 52, 53, 54, 56, 58, 60, 61, 67, 70, 77, 78, 79, 84, 86, 87, 88, 90, 91
dollar costs, 74
Drug Enforcement Administration (DEA), 66
drug trafficking, 9

E

early retirement, 82
echoing, 48
economies of scale, 35
electronic communications, 93
electronic surveillance, 91, 92, 93, 94, 95
embassy, 83
employees, 65, 76
employers, 83
employment, 39, 65, 89
encryption, 72, 82
endurance, 41
enemies, 40
energy, 68
enforcement, 67, 68, 85
engineering, 48
environment(s), 30, 32, 56, 70, 82, 83
equipment, 31, 32, 57
everyday life, 34
evidence, 83, 95
evolution, 31, 39
execution, 13, 15, 17, 20, 25
executive branch, x, 32, 33, 46, 56, 57, 63, 74, 95
executive order(s), 77, 90, 91
exercise, 12
expertise, 39, 48, 84
exploitation, 41, 44, 47
extremists, 74

F

Federal Bureau of Investigation (FBI), 13, 24, 66, 67, 68, 71, 73, 76, 77, 87, 89, 90, 97
federal government, 71
Feingold, Senator Russ, 16
fiber, 48, 71
fidelity, 34
financial, 46
FISA, 91, 92, 93, 94, 95
force, 19, 43, 47, 48, 93
foreign intelligence, 70, 71, 85, 92, 93, 94
foreign language, 21, 84
foreign person, 92
Fort Hood, xi, 64, 76, 97, 98
funding, viii, ix, 2, 3, 5, 7, 10, 13, 15, 16, 18, 19, 23, 24, 25, 28, 30, 36, 41, 45, 49, 52, 53, 58, 65, 73, 78
funds, vii, 3, 4, 5, 13, 14, 15, 17, 18, 25, 35, 38, 46, 52, 56, 81, 87, 88, 90
fusion, 71

G

GAO, 37, 38, 39, 42, 48, 49, 50, 58, 59, 60, 69, 81, 98, 99
GDP, 4, 5, 7
GPS, 34
grants, 51
graph, 7
groupthink, 73
growth, vii, x, 1, 7, 9, 19, 29, 30, 35, 42, 52, 63, 78, 79
guidance, 10, 12, 68
guidelines, 84, 88

H

hiring, 78
history, 40, 43, 61
homeland security, 56
House, 10, 11, 17, 18, 19, 21, 23, 24, 25, 38, 43, 45, 46, 50, 52, 53, 54, 57, 58, 60, 61, 65, 69, 71, 79, 80, 81, 87, 88, 89, 91, 93, 94, 95, 98
House of Representatives, 25, 57, 58, 60, 61, 95
human, 3, 57, 64, 65, 67, 72, 78, 82, 83, 84, 89
human right(s), 84

I

identification, 47
image(s), 47
imagery, 35, 36, 39, 43, 45, 47, 82, 83
immunity, 93, 95
improvements, 9
individuals, 76, 84, 94
industry, 36, 39, 59, 84
inflation, 7, 23
information sharing, x, xi, 64, 69, 70
information technology, xi, 64, 76
infrastructure, 35
innovator, 72
institution building, x, 63
institutional change, 71
institutional reforms, 77
institutions, x, 64
integration, 47
intelligence programs, vii, 1, 14, 15, 18, 21, 48, 56, 68, 86, 87, 99
Intelligence Reform, x, 10, 14, 15, 22, 25, 63, 65, 67, 69, 70, 72, 73, 77, 85, 86, 87, 88, 91, 95
Intelligence Reform and Terrorism Prevention Act, x, 10, 14, 22, 25, 63, 65, 69, 70, 95
intelligence spending, vii, 1, 3, 5, 6, 7, 8, 9, 14, 23, 24, 64, 86, 87
international communication, 94
international law, 76
interoperability, 48
investment(s), x, 21, 28, 30, 35, 40, 46, 55
Iran, 73, 75
Iraq, 12, 24, 30, 31, 32, 40, 43, 44, 47, 50, 51, 57, 70, 71, 73, 75, 96
Iron Curtain, 35
isolation, 39, 46
ISR systems, ix, x, 27, 28, 29, 30, 31, 32, 33, 41, 44, 52, 54, 55, 56, 57
issues, vii, viii, ix, x, xi, 2, 3, 9, 19, 27, 28, 32, 47, 48, 50, 52, 53, 54, 55, 63, 64, 66, 68, 69, 71, 73, 74, 76, 84, 85, 88

J

judicial branch, 94
judiciary, 94
Judiciary Committee, 92
jurisdiction, 17, 22, 52, 81, 87

K

Kosovo, 31

L

landscape, 32
language skills, 73, 84
law enforcement, 67, 68, 70, 76, 85
leadership, x, 34, 63, 91
leaks, 69
Lebanon, 40
legislation, x, 14, 17, 18, 22, 31, 38, 51, 52, 53, 63, 65, 68, 69, 73, 80, 86, 88, 90, 91, 92, 95, 99
legislative proposals, 90
light, x, 9, 12, 28, 55, 71, 77, 84, 91, 97
Louisiana, 25

M

magnitude, 8, 9
majority, 6, 45, 52, 79
man, 42

management, xi, 10, 17, 38, 64, 67, 78, 88
Marine Corps, 13, 66
maritime security, 68
materials, 24, 85
matter, 41, 73
McCain, Senator John, 54
measurement, 84
media, 3, 35, 39, 43, 74, 75, 76, 78, 80, 83, 91, 92
methodology, 6, 8
military, vii, ix, xi, 1, 3, 4, 5, 6, 12, 13, 24, 27, 28, 29, 30, 32, 33, 34, 37, 39, 40, 43, 46, 49, 53, 54, 55, 57, 64, 67, 68, 71, 72, 76, 82, 83, 84, 85, 87, 88
MIP, viii, 2, 4, 5, 6, 13, 23, 33, 46, 86, 88
mission(s), 29, 32, 35, 38, 43, 44, 47, 48, 51, 56, 58, 59, 67, 66, 68, 70, 71, 77, 78
modernization, 92
modifications, 91
multiple nodes, 39

N

narcotics, 83, 84
nation states, 55, 72
National Aeronautics and Space Administration, 45
National Counterterrorism Center (NCTC), 16, 77, 86, 90, 98, 99
National Defense Authorization Act, 18, 54, 58, 60, 61, 78
National Intelligence Program, vii, 1, 3, 15, 16, 18, 22, 23, 25, 33, 46, 64, 86, 87, 88, 90
national policy, ix, 27, 33, 52
national security, xi, 6, 10, 37, 38, 46, 49, 53, 57, 64, 67, 69, 73, 84, 94
National Security Agency, 13, 30, 66, 67
National Security Council, 33, 56
National Strategy, 80
NCTC, 77
NIP, vii, viii, 1, 2, 3, 4, 5, 6, 11, 12, 13, 14, 15, 16, 17, 18, 19, 23, 25, 33, 46, 64, 86, 87, 89
NOAA, 45
Northwest Airlines, 97
NSA, 3, 13, 30, 66, 67, 82, 87, 88, 91
nuclear program, 73
nuclear weapons, 68

O

Obama, 32, 41, 50, 51, 58, 60, 81, 98
Obama Administration, 32, 41, 50, 51, 81
objectivity, 73
Office of Management and Budget, 14, 24, 56, 88, 99
officials, vii, 2, 3, 10, 38, 46, 48, 59, 64, 68, 78, 83, 84, 85, 89
OMB, 14
Operation Iraqi Freedom, 71
operations, ix, xi, 4, 5, 12, 27, 29, 30, 31, 32, 33, 34, 37, 39, 40, 43, 45, 48, 49, 50, 51, 55, 57, 64, 67, 72, 78, 82, 85, 90, 91
opportunities, 35
orbit, 33, 39
outsourcing, 82
overlap, 31, 34, 41, 46, 83
oversight, ix, x, 10, 12, 18, 19, 20, 21, 25, 27, 28, 31, 33, 36, 43, 49, 52, 57, 63, 66, 73, 75, 76, 80, 81, 87, 88, 91, 92, 93

P

PAA, 92
Pakistan, 75, 76
parallel, 11, 45, 54
peace, 31
peacekeeping, 31
Pentagon, 45, 57, 59, 65, 89
permit, 21, 42, 79, 92
Persian Gulf War, 71
personal relationship, 78
physical features, 83
platform, 44
policy, 11, 16, 34, 51, 70, 80
policy makers, 11, 16
policy reform, 80
policymakers, ix, 28, 29, 30, 32, 33, 46, 67, 89, 98

political party, 20
portfolio, 32
preparation, 10, 16, 20, 30, 65, 78
preparedness, 89
President, x, 4, 5, 7, 12, 14, 17, 24, 28, 30, 33, 45, 53, 55, 60, 65, 67, 69, 71, 79, 80, 87, 88, 90, 91, 95
President Clinton, 79
price index, 4
principles, 51
prior knowledge, 83
private sector, 44, 83
procurement, 30, 31, 32, 36, 38, 52, 55, 74
producers, 10
professionals, 21, 45, 65
programming, 11, 37
proliferation, 48, 69, 82
protection, 54
public concern, viii, 2
purchasing power, 23

Q

qualifications, 45, 84

R

radio, 84
real terms, 6, 24
real time, 75
reality, 34
recall, 9
recognition, 59
recommendations, 19, 20, 21, 22, 50, 53, 59, 60, 65, 89, 90
redundancy, x, 64, 69, 70
reform(s), viii, 2, 12, 15, 19, 60, 65, 66, 67, 70, 72, 73, 76, 77, 85, 86, 87, 88, 90, 91
regulations, 47
reliability, 43
requirements, ix, 10, 15, 28, 30, 31, 32, 35, 36, 37, 38, 40, 41, 42, 43, 45, 46, 48, 49, 53, 55, 69, 83, 84, 93, 94
resistance, 18
resolution, 14, 21, 39
resource allocation, 49
resources, 9, 11, 14, 43, 45, 49, 71, 72, 79
response, x, 10, 25, 28, 43, 55, 65, 81, 86, 89, 95
restrictions, 80
retirement, 25, 83
risk(s), xi, 35, 46, 50, 64, 76, 84

S

satellite service, 35
satellite technology, 36
savings, 39
science, 72
scope, 77
Secretary of Defense, viii, 2, 4, 10, 15, 31, 37, 41, 43, 44, 45, 48, 51, 53, 54, 57, 58, 59, 60, 67, 73, 77, 86, 88
security, xi, 32, 45, 64, 68, 85
Senate, x, 9, 17, 18, 19, 21, 22, 23, 24, 25, 26, 28, 36, 39, 43, 49, 53, 54, 55, 58, 61, 65, 69, 70, 71, 77, 78, 79, 80, 81, 86, 87, 88, 89, 90, 92, 93, 94, 95, 96, 97, 98
sensitivity, 73
sensors, 35, 39, 42, 47, 48, 84
September 11, vii, viii, 1, 2, 6, 9, 23, 65, 74, 89, 90, 94, 95
services, 29, 35, 40, 42, 43, 50, 52, 53, 54, 56, 57, 68, 76, 86, 87
shape, 9, 10, 56
signals, 30, 43, 67, 82
solution, 39, 46
Soviet Union, 9, 10, 82
specifications, 48
speech, 59, 60
spending, vii, viii, 1, 2, 3, 5, 6, 7, 8, 9, 10, 14, 17, 23, 24, 54, 64, 68, 86, 87
stability, 21, 32, 34
stabilization, 31
stakeholders, 38
state(s), 9, 32, 51, 68, 74, 77, 81, 93
statutes, 47, 79
statutory provisions, 79
strategic planning, 31, 82
structure, 17, 18, 20, 25, 45, 51, 85

submarines, 82
substitutes, 75
surveillance, viii, 27, 29, 33, 37, 43, 47, 50, 52, 54, 55, 56, 57, 83, 90, 91, 92, 94, 95
synchronize, 39

T

tanks, ix, 28, 29
target, 31, 34, 37, 45, 82, 93, 94
Task Force, 24, 41, 50, 51, 59, 60
teams, 98
techniques, ix, 28
technology(s), viii, ix, 27, 28, 29, 30, 34, 35, 36, 39, 41, 42, 44, 46, 49, 51, 55, 71, 82, 92, 94
telecommunications, 93, 95
telephone, 35
temperament, 78
tension, 34
terrorism, 9, 71, 72, 77, 85, 86, 89, 98
terrorist activities, 88
terrorist attack, vii, 1, 3, 74, 89, 90, 98
terrorist groups, 29, 55, 72, 82, 83, 84
terrorists, 65, 89, 95
testing, 46
The Homeland Security Act, 68, 77, 85
theatre, 43
threats, viii, 2, 8, 9, 65, 68, 77, 85
time constraints, 49
time frame, 72
Title V, 16
trade-off, 34
training, 21, 59, 84
transformation, 77
translation, 85
transparency, 17, 19, 25, 74
Treasury, 13, 14, 17, 24, 68, 88

U

U.S. policy, 76
unit cost, 59
United, viii, 2, 9, 10, 22, 24, 29, 32, 41, 45, 57, 59, 60, 61, 65, 75, 76, 77, 85, 89, 91, 92, 93, 94, 95, 96, 97, 98, 99
United States, viii, 2, 9, 10, 22, 24, 32, 41, 45, 57, 59, 60, 61, 65, 75, 76, 77, 85, 89, 91, 92, 93, 94, 95, 96, 97, 98, 99
unmanned aerial vehicles, ix, 28, 42, 75, 82
urban, 32
urban areas, 32
USA, 44, 70, 85
USA Patriot Act, 70
USA PATRIOT Act, 85

V

varieties, 16
vehicles, ix, 28, 41, 42, 75, 82
Vietnam, 40
violent extremist, 32
vote, 21, 65, 81, 95

W

war, 38, 70
warning systems, 69
Washington, vii, ix, 1, 3, 24, 28, 29, 38, 58, 59, 60, 61, 98
waste, x, 39, 64, 69
wealth, 72
weapons, 29, 40, 44, 67, 70, 73, 75
weapons of mass destruction, 29, 70, 73, 75
White House, 58, 69, 70, 80, 88, 97
WikiLeaks, xi, 64
wiretaps, 95
witnesses, 90
WMD, 73
workforce, x, 28, 55, 65, 79
World Trade Center, 65, 89
World War I, 44

Y

Yemen, 76
yield, 30, 34